General Editor

SWINBURNE

WW

SWINBURNE

Catherine Maxwell

© Copyright 2006 by Catherine Maxwell

First published in 2006 by Northcote House Publishers Ltd, Horndon, Tavistock, Devon, PL19 9NQ, United Kingdom.
Tel: +44 (01822) 810066. Fax: +44 (01822) 810034.

British Library Cataloguing-in-Publication Data
A catalogue record for this book is available from the British Library

ISBN 0-7463-1106-0 hardcover
ISBN 0-7463-0969-4 paperback

Typeset by TW Typesetting, Plymouth, Devon
Printed and bound in the United Kingdom by Athenaeum Press Ltd., Gateshead

Gosse, *Life*   Edmund Gosse, *The Life of Algernon Charles Swin-burne* (London: Macmillan, 1917)

Rooksby   Rikky Rooksby, *A. C. Swinburne: A Poet's Life* (Aldershot: Scolar Press, 1997)

Many of the principal poems examined can also be found in the editions by Binyon, Findlay and Maxwell listed in the Bibliography. References to 'Notes on Poems and Reviews' are to both Haynes (in which the essay is reprinted in Appendix 1) and *SR*.

References and Abbreviations

AYL   *A Year's Letters*, ed. Francis Jacques Sypher (London: Peter Owen, 1976)

ES   *Essays and Studies* (London: Chatto & Windus, 1875)

Haynes   *Poems and Ballads & Atalanta in Calydon*, ed. Kenneth Haynes (Harmondsworth: Penguin, 2000)

LB   *Lesbia Brandon*, ed. Randolph Hughes (London: Falcon Press, 1952)

Letters   *The Swinburne Letters*, ed. Cecil Y. Lang, 6 vols. (New Haven: Yale University Press, 1959–62)

PS   *The Poems of Algernon Charles Swinburne*, 6 vols. (London: Chatto & Windus, 1904)

SAC   *Swinburne as Critic*, ed. Clyde K. Hyder (London and Boston: Routledge & Kegan Paul, 1972)

SCH   Clyde K. Hyder (ed.), *Swinburne: The Critical Heritage* (London: Routledge & Kegan Paul, 1970)

SR   *Swinburne Replies: Notes on Poems and Reviews, Under the Microscope, Dedicatory Epistle*, ed. Clyde K. Hyder (Syracuse, NY: Syracuse University Press, 1966)

SS   'Simeon Solomon: Notes on his "Vision of Love" ' (1871), reprinted in *The Complete Works of Algernon Charles Swinburne*, ed. Edmund Gosse and Thomas J. Wise, 20 vols. (The Bonchurch Edition; London and New York: William Heinemann and Gabriel Wells, 1925–7), xvi (1926)

WB   *William Blake: A Critical Essay*, 2nd edn. (London: John Camden Hotten, 1868)

1899   Publishes *Rosamund, Queen of the Lombards*.

1903   Suffers first attack of pneumonia.

1904   Publishes *A Channel Passage and Other Poems*.

1905   Publishes *Love's Cross-Currents*. Watts-Dunton marries his secretary, Clara Reich.

1907   Refuses honorary degree from Oxford.

1908   Publishes *The Age of Shakespeare* and *The Duke of Gandia*.

1909   Dies from pneumonia on 10 April at The Pines. Buried 15 April at Bonchurch, Isle of Wight.

between Rossetti and Swinburne ends because of Rossetti's ill health.

1874   Publishes *Bothwell: A Tragedy*.

1875   Publishes *George Chapman: A Critical Essay*, *Songs of Two Nations* and *Essays and Studies*.

1876   Publishes his second classical verse drama, *Erectheus: A Tragedy*.

1877   Publishes *A Note on Charlotte Brontë*. Admiral Swinburne dies. Unchecked by his father, Swinburne sinks further into alcoholism. Epistolary novel *A Year's Letters* (later known as *Love's Cross-Currents*) published in serial form.

1878   Publishes *Poems and Ballads: Second Series*.

1879   In June Theodore Watts (Watts-Dunton after 1896), at the request of the poet's mother, takes Swinburne, now severely ill from alcoholism, from his London lodgings to Putney, and then to Holmwood. In September, Swinburne moves into No. 2 The Pines with Watts, where he spends the rest of his life.

1880   Publishes *Songs of the Springtides*, *Studies in Song* and *The Heptalogia*.

1881   Publishes *Mary Stuart: A Tragedy*.

1882   Publishes *Tristram of Lyonesse and Other Poems*. Visits Hugo in Paris accompanied by Watts.

1883   Publishes *A Century of Roundels*.

1884   Publishes *A Midsummer Holiday and Other Poems*.

1885   Publishes drama *Marino Faliero*.

1886   Publishes essays *Miscellanies* and *A Study of Victor Hugo*.

1887   Publishes *Locrine: A Tragedy* and *Whitmania*.

1888   Attacks Whistler in an article 'Mr Whistler's Lecture on Art'.

1889   Publishes *Poems and Ballads: Third Series*.

1892   Publishes *The Sisters: A Tragedy* (contemporary drama). Gen. Disney Leith dies.

1893   Mary Disney Leith visits and corresponds.

1894   Publishes *Astrophel and Other Poems* and *Studies in Prose and Poetry*.

1896   Publishes *The Tale of Balen*. Swinburne's mother dies.

1860 Returns to Oxford and passes Classics examination (May), but leaves after withdrawing from his Finals. Moves to London and publishes his verse-plays *Rosamond* and *The Queen Mother*.

1861 Visits Mentone and Italy. Given pension of £400 p.a. by his father to pursue a literary career in London. Starts important friendships with Richard Monckton Milnes (later Lord Houghton) and the explorer Richard Burton.

1862 Publishes poetry and essays in the *Spectator*, including his review of Baudelaire's *Les Fleurs du mal*.

1863 Takes up residence with Rossetti at Tudor House, Cheyne Walk, Chelsea. Develops close friendship with the painter Simeon Solomon. Visits Paris with Whistler. His favourite sister Edith dies. Stays with his cousin Mary Gordon and her family on the Isle of Wight and begins *Atalanta in Calydon*.

1864 Travels in Italy and meets Landor, one of his poetic heroes. Leaves Tudor House. Mary Gordon announces her engagement to Col. Disney Leith.

1865 Publication of *Atalanta in Calydon* in March. Swinburne's family move to Holmwood, Oxfordshire. Mary Gordon marries in June. Publication of *Chastelard: A Tragedy* in November.

1866 *Poems and Ballads* published by Moxon, withdrawn, and then republished by John Camden Hotten. 'Notes on Poems and Reviews' published to address the critical furore.

1867 Meets Mazzini and is encouraged to write poems for the cause of Italian liberty. Starts brief affair with the actress and poet Adah Menken in late November/early December; it lasts about six months.

1868 Publishes *William Blake: A Critical Essay*.

1871 Publishes *Songs before Sunrise*. Severe illness resulting from alcoholism. His father removes him to Holmwood to recuperate.

1872 Returns to London and replies to Robert Buchanan's attack on himself and Rossetti ('The Fleshly School of Poetry') in *Under the Microscope*. The relationship

Biographical Outline

1836	Marriage of Capt. Charles Henry Swinburne and Lady Jane Hamilton.
1837	Algernon Charles Swinburne born on 5 April, at 7 Chester Street, Grosvernor Place, London, the eldest of six children.
1848	Swinburne prepared for Eton by Revd Foster Fenwick, Vicar of Brook, Isle of Wight.
1849	Arrives at Eton. Writes four-act tragedy 'The Unhappy Revenge'. Visits Wordsworth at Rydal Mount with parents.
1852	Wins Prince Consort's Prize for Modern Languages.
1853	Leaves Eton. Sent to Cambo, Northumberland, to be prepared for Oxford by Revd John Wilkinson.
1854	Parents veto his request to become a cavalry officer.
1855	Tutored by Revd Russell Woodford, Kempsford, Glos. Visits Germany with his uncle.
1856	Enters Balliol College, Oxford, on 23 Jan. Becomes member of the Old Mortality Society, an intellectual group founded by John Nichol.
1857	Publishes essays and poems in *Undergraduate Papers*, the monthly journal of Old Mortality. His poem 'The Temple of Janus' fails to win the Newdigate poetry prize. Meets Morris, Jones and D. G. Rossetti at work decorating the Oxford Union.
1858	Visits Tennyson at Farringford in January. Takes a second in Moderations and wins the Taylorian Scholarship for French and Italian in June.
1859	Fails Classics examination and sent to read modern history with Revd William Stubbs, Navestock, Essex.

Acknowledgements

I would like to take this opportunity of thanking the Harry Ransom Research Center of the University of Texas at Austin for awarding me a scholarship that enabled me to work with their Swinburne manuscript and book collections during April 2002. My especial thanks to HRC Director Tom Staley, to Debbie Armstrong, and to Pat Fox, Head of Library Circulation, for helping to make my stay such a productive one, and also to Professor Roger Louis for giving me the opportunity to speak on Swinburne at the HRC British Studies seminar. I would also like to express my great gratitude to Stefano Evangelista, Paul Hamilton, Patricia Pulham and Sarah Wood, for reading and commenting on various draft chapters of this book, to Matt Cook and Ivan Crozier for points of information concerning male homosexuality and criminality in the nineteenth century, and to Mike Edwards and Ros Allen for information about Greek tragedy and Arthurian literature. My thanks also to Hilary Walford, my copy-editor. Finally I should like to acknowledge Catherine Trippett at Random House for advice concerning Swinburne's copyright, and the British Library for permission to print a transcription of 'Pasiphae'.

Contents

For Patricia Pulham
and Sarah Wood

Altogether I think we ought to read only books that bite and sting us. If the book we are reading doesn't shake us awake like a blow on the skull, why bother reading it in the first place? . . . A book must be the axe for the frozen sea within us. That is what I believe.

(Franz Kafka to Oskar Pollak, 1904)

Introduction

In October 1866 *The Englishwoman's Domestic Magazine* published 'Incognita', a light-hearted poem by Austin Dobson, in which a self-mocking narrator ruefully tells how he falls for the charms of an unchaperoned young woman whom he meets on the train. Taking full advantage of the opportunity to meet members of the opposite sex without formal introduction, both parties settle down to a conversation in which the narrator is captivated by the apparently artless chatter of his companion. Their talk turns to literature and poetry in particular, and, although 'Incognita', the young woman, is smugly patronized by the narrator for her failure to appreciate Browning, we note her keenness to show that she is *au fait* with the contemporary literary scene:

> 'Like Browning?' 'But so-so.' His proof lay
> Too deep for her frivolous mood,
> That preferred your mere metrical *soufflé*
> To the stronger poetical food.
> Yet at times he was good – 'as a tonic';
> Was Tennyson writing just now?
> And was this new poet Byronic,
> And clever and naughty, or how?

(ll. 25–32)

The 'new poet' was, of course, Algernon Charles Swinburne (1837–1909), who in 1865 had published his acclaimed classical epic *Atalanta in Calydon* and who, in the latter part of 1866, was experiencing notoriety as the author of the scandalous *Poems and Ballads*. This collection, published in July by Moxon and then speedily withdrawn in August, had been republished in

1

September by the considerably less respectable firm of John Camden Hotten to a storm of critical disapproval. Reflecting the popular feeling that here was a new force in English poetry, Dobson's 'Incognita' instinctively groups the new-comer with the older, more established Tennyson and Browning, as well as identifying him with Byron – in his own day the controversial subject of a *succès du scandale*. Indeed, Swinburne himself would complain that he had 'been more be-written and belied than any man since Byron' (*Letters*, iii. 12).

That Swinburne was immediately recognized as a serious challenger for poetic laurels seems indisputable. Swinburne's most recent biographer, Rikky Rooksby, cites a letter written in October 1866, the same month as Dobson's poem was published, by the historian W. H. E. Lecky: 'A very great poet has arisen in England – Algernon Swinburne – who stands apart from all his predecessors, and is probably destined to exercise a most profound influence on the ways of thought of English-men for many years to come. All literary London is now ringing with the genius, the blasphemies and indecencies of his last book' (Rooksby, 141).

In an age where poets were the celebrities of their day, Swinburne's activities were a topic of perennial interest. During the early part of his career in particular and up to the close of the 1870s he was the subject of gossip, intrigue and speculation. In early 1868, when he was conducting his brief liaison with the American actress and poet Adah Menken, photographs of the couple soon found their way into the shops for sale and were widely displayed throughout London, much to the consternation of Swinburne's family. On 10 July 1868, when he fainted in the Reading Room of the British Museum, the matter was reported in the newspapers the next day. Edmund Gosse, seeing him carried out, 'recognised him instantly from his photographs which now filled the shop windows' (*Life*, 178). In male literary circles and in the gentlemen's clubs Swinburne's susceptibility to alcohol – even very small quantities of liquor could induce inebriation and riotous behaviour that he was unable to recall when sober – was well known and stories abounded of his drunken antics and unlicensed outbursts. Some of this talk was almost certainly exaggerated and the poet was perfectly capable of appearing in other lights. An American commentator, Lucy Fountain, describing a *soirée* she spent in Swinburne's company in September 1870, sounds faintly disappointed: 'The rampant lion of who we had heard so much was, if anything, rather more quiet and gentlemanly and soft-spoken (even after the wine) than any one there.'[1] However, until his removal from the central London scene in 1879 by his friend the solicitor and critic Theodore Watts (Watts-Dunton after 1896), Swinburne was seen by some of his more roistering associates as a daredevil Dionysiac, always up for fun. The truth was much less glamorous: the poet was isolated, depressed and dangerously ill. Removed to the safety of Putney, he was nursed back to health and, there, out of the glare of publicity, spent the last thirty years of his life, tranquilly pursuing his writing, under the watchful eye of Watts, who monitored his visitors, winnowing out what he took to be the more disruptive of his friends and associates.

Although Swinburne's life became quieter, his reputation as a poet continued to remain high. In January 1886 the young Arthur Symons opened an article in the *London Quarterly Review* with the words: 'If almost any ordinary person should be asked the question, who, in your opinion, are the principal poets now living in England? one might safely suppose that he would name, without hesitation, though perhaps in a different order, Browning, Tennyson, Swinburne.'[2] In their *The Victorian Age of English Literature* published in 1892, Margaret and F. R. Oliphant referred to Swinburne as 'this great contemporary poet, who is probably destined to take the first place in English poetry when the career of the present Patriarch is over', and, when Tennyson died that year, the same view was expressed by Queen Victoria, who announced to Gladstone: 'I am told Mr Swinburne is the best poet in my dominions.'[3] But Gladstone was of the opinion that Swinburne's republican sentiments, expressed in his radical collection *Songs before Sunrise* (1871), made him an unsuitable candidate. The decision was deferred for some time, but when twenty-two leading literary figures of the day were polled for their opinion by *The Idler* in April 1895, twelve out of the nineteen who expressed a preference thought Swinburne should be selected, the next nearest candidate being

Kipling with two votes. Oscar Wilde's gracefully expressed opinion is worth quoting: 'Mr Swinburne is already the Poet Laureate of England. The fact that his appointment to this high post has not been degraded by official confirmation renders his position all the more unassailable. He whom all poets love is the Laureate Poet always.'[4] In the end the post, somewhat farcically, went to the comparatively minor figure of Alfred Austin, now memorable only for his attacks on poets more gifted than himself. Edmund Gosse, a member of the English selection committee for the Nobel Prize, also tells how for 'years and years' the committee unanimously recommended Swinburne, and 'were annually and finally snubbed by seeing it given to Kipling whom nobody had recommended'.[5]

Although by the time he died in April 1909 in his Putney retreat Swinburne had long been out of the public eye, he was still understood to be the dominant influence in English poetry by the rising generation of young poets. T. S. Eliot, reflecting on the early stages of his friend Ezra Pound's career in the first decade of the twentieth century, commented: 'The question was still: where do we go from Swinburne? and the answer appeared to be, nowhere.' *Poems and Ballads* (1866) had proved to be one of the most influential verse collections of the nineteenth century, leaving its evident mark on the poets of the Victorian *fin de siècle* such as Symons, Wilde, Ernest Dowson, A. Mary F. Robinson and Amy Levy. As Pound would ask rather testily in his *ABC of Reading*: 'Did the "90s" add anything to English poetry, or did they merely prune Swinburne?'[6] Pound, Eliot, Yeats and their *confrères* applied themselves to the task of freeing themselves from Swinburne, a labour they performed chiefly through acts of hostility, aggression and disavowal, in marked contrast to women poets such as H.D. and Edith Sitwell, who seemed better able to admire and innovate at the same time.

Today in spite of being increasingly understood as a major influence on nineteenth-century *fin-de-siècle* literature and on twentieth-century Modernism, Swinburne still lacks even a small portion of the attention given to his two older contemporaries Tennyson and Browning. The reasons for this neglect are complex, but a major factor may be the many kinds of caricature levelled at the poet throughout his career and afterwards. Surprising though it at first sounds, caricature and neglect are linked in that an individual who is the object of much caricature tends not to have his achievements taken seriously. Caricature tends to diminish, to cut the subject down to size and make him or her more manageable. It most frequently appears to be a defensive measure in that it suggests that the subject's importance and talents should not be overvalued or held in high esteem. Swinburne is, I think, a particularly interesting case, in that it is hard to think of another nineteenth-century poet who was so relentlessly caricatured, especially, in a very literal sense, with regard to his appearance. Swinburne was physically small and slight, physical characteristics that unfortunately complement the diminishing function of caricature. Max Beerbohm's famous cartoons of the Pre-Raphaelite circle depict a tiny Swinburne surrounded by the considerably larger, if not to say, massively fleshy forms of his peers. Add to this physical slightness a shock of red hair, a seemingly large head on a proportionally smaller body, a voice that became high pitched when excited, and a surfeit of nervous energy that communicated itself in jerks and twitchiness, and you have a set of characteristics ripe for comic exploitation. Beerbohm reproduces some of these characteristics in his much later humorous essay 'No. 2 The Pines' (1920) about visiting the elderly Swinburne at his house in Putney:

> Here he was . . . a strange small figure in grey, having an air at once noble and roguish, proud and skittish. . . . Sparse and straggling though the grey hair that fringed the immense pale dome of his head, and venerably haloed though he was for me by his greatness, there was yet about him something – boyish? girlish? childish, rather; something of a beautifully well-bred child. But he had the eyes of a god, and the smile of an elf. . . . His hands were tiny, even for his size, and they fluttered helplessly, touchingly, unceasingly. (*SCH* 237–8)

Swinburne was quite frequently referred to as 'little Swinburne' by his friends and associates and, while this is undoubtedly often a term of affection, it might also be seen as a form of diminishment. Edmund Gosse, Swinburne's first biographer, who got to know him well in the 1870s, admired

5

him greatly, but his underlying resentment at the poet's superior literary gifts reveals itself in a vein of mockery and disparagement that runs through his writings. His *Encyclopaedia Britannica* article (1911) on Swinburne is startling in its ambivalence, and throughout his writings on the poet, especially in his essay in *Portraits and Sketches* (1912), he seems to go out of his way to focus on Swinburne's eccentricities and unconventional appearance:

> occasionally when I have parted from him in the evening after saying 'Good-night', he has simply sat back in the deep sofa in his sitting-room, his little feet close together, his arms against his side, folded in his frock-coat like a grass-hopper in its wing-covers, and fallen asleep . . .

> His vast brain seemed to weigh down and give solidity to a frame otherwise as light as thistledown, a body almost as immaterial as that of a fairy.

> He was like that little geyser in Iceland which is always simmering, but which, if it is irritated by having pieces of turf thrown into it, instantly boils over and flings its menacing column at the sky.[7]

Gosse seems to have been responsible for introducing a tongue-in-cheek, overblown style of writing about Swinburne, which has been unfortunately influential. Tennyson and Browning had their detractors, but it is hard to imagine them being represented in this arch, belittling way by their biographers.

The physical caricatures were not just restricted to cartoons or anecdotal essays but entered literary criticism, where the strangeness of the poet's body became merged with the body of his work. In his biography of Swinburne, Gosse launched the influential trope of the pagan invader assaulting Victorian proprieties. Mid-Victorian British poetry, says Gosse, was a serene and 'beautifully guarded park. . . . Into this quiet park, to the infinite alarm of the fallow-deer, a young Bacchus was now preparing to burst, in the company of a troop of Maenads, and to the accompaniment of cymbals and clattering kettle-drums' (*Life*, 135–6). This image became hard for subsequent commentators to resist. Even the judicious T. E. Welby, writing in 1926 about the publication of Swinburne's controversial verses *Poems and Ballads*, followed suit: 'He broke in upon that rather agreeably tedious Victorian tea-party with the effect of some pagan creature, at once impish and divine, leaping on to the sleek lawn, to stamp its goat-foot in challenge, to deride with its screech of laughter the admirable decorum of the conversation.'[8] Then we have Peter Quennell writing in 1949 about the same event: 'With his aureole of flaming hair, his feverishly dancing limbs and perpetually fluttering hands, that prodigious youth had burst through the enchanted forest, the Tennysonian Broceliande of late-Romantic poetry, to the shrilling of bacchic flutes and of corybantic cymbals.'[9] Here the exotic, alien, physical extraordinariness of the poet is one with his poetry, while the 'bacchic' references do not just refer to the pagan affront and the sensuality of *Poems and Ballads* but hint at Swinburne's propensity to drink and dissolute behaviour. The received view of Swinburne has always been informed by cartoonish accounts of his personal life. Certainly various aspects of it do lend themselves readily to caricature: the somewhat incongruous affair with Adah Menken, the preference for flagellation in the brothels of St John's Wood and the sudden reversal into suburban gentility. All these things are part and parcel of Swinburne's life and worthy of comment, but the danger is that overemphasis on Swinburne's idiosyncrasies has helped overshadow a serious appreciation of the poetry. It is interesting that even today the cartoon Swinburne is seen as an acceptable representative for the poet. In its recent 2002 reissue of L. M. Findlay's edition of Swinburne's *Selected Poems* (1982), Carcanet Press has chosen to replace the jacket image – formerly R. P. Staples's National Portrait Gallery image of an older sage-like Swinburne – with Carlo Pellegrini's caricature 'Songs before Sunrise' (also from the National Portrait Gallery), as if a serious portrait and a caricature were interchangeable. Again it is hard to imagine another leading nineteenth-century poet's work being presented in this way.

In addition to caricatures of the poet's appearance, his life and habits, there is a third and final kind of caricature and parody – that which is levelled specifically at the verse. The early critics, outraged by Swinburne's subject matter, caricatured the poet as decadent and deviant, using, as we have seen Gosse did later, images associated with classical antiquity. John Morley wrote of Swinburne in the infamous first review of *Poems and Ballads*: 'He is either the vindictive and scornful apostle of a crushing iron-shod despair, or else he is the libidinous laureate of a pack of satyrs.' Swinburne, he says, 'has revealed to the world a mind all aflame with the feverish carnality of a schoolboy over the dirtiest passages in Lemprière' (*SCH* 29, 23).[10] For Robert Buchanan, Swinburne is Gito (a homosexual youth in Petronius's *Satyricon*) 'seated in the tub of Diogenes, conscious of the filth and whining at the stars' (*SCH* 32). For these mid-Victorian critics the issue was with content: Swinburne was undoubtedly talented, but his blasphemous and sexually provocative subjects put him beyond the pale. Yet, if early critics were bothered by the content of these poems, later critics, perhaps in a bid to prove themselves more sophisticated than their Victorian forebears, defended themselves against the verse by claiming that there was nothing there. So began a process of emptying Swinburne out and new caricatures came into being. Swinburne's sonorous lyricism and metrical fluency were deemed by his detractors to be all sound and precious little sense. There is no real content, they suggested, he is only a mellifluous and monotonous singer; he is technically brilliant, but he has nothing to say, or, if there is something there, it is something that can be appreciated only by the very young. Swinburne's reputation suffered badly during the first half of the twentieth century, when it became fashionable to deride Victorian poetry and when a liking for Swinburne was assumed to be a fad of impressionable youth, something to be grown out of as one developed more mature literary tastes. T. S. Eliot was probably most influential in ensuring Swinburne's neglect when, in his essay 'Swinburne as Poet' (1920), he damned the poet with faint praise. Promoting the view that Swinburne's verse is predominantly a matter of wordplay, he managed to suggest that the world of the poems is completely self-referential and inward-looking, and thus of limited appeal. His essay concludes with a typical back-handed compliment:

> Only a man of genius could dwell so exclusively and consistently among words as Swinburne. His language is not, like the language of bad poetry, dead. It is very much alive, with this singular life of its own. But the language which is more important to us is that

which is struggling to digest and express new objects, new groups of objects, new aspects, as, for instance, the prose of Mr James Joyce or the earlier Conrad.[11]

Swinburne's poetry is at the same time selectively praised and consigned to the lumber room. It is not, Eliot intimates, of interest to the present moment. Later, in a review of his friend Ezra Pound's *Personae* in *The Dial* for January 1928, Eliot was more direct: 'Swinburne's form is uninteresting, because he is literally saying next to nothing, and unless you mean something with your words they will do nothing for you.'[12]

If, because of the disdain of Eliot and his followers Swinburne went out of favour for the first part of the twentieth century, his star began to rise in the second half. Caricature began to give way in the face of informed opinion. This was mainly due to the scholarly efforts of Cecil Y. Lang, editor of the invaluable six-volume *Swinburne Letters* in 1959–62 and *New Writings by Swinburne* (1964), and C. K. Hyder, editor of *Swinburne Replies* (1966), three essays in which Swinburne took on his Victorian critics, and *Swinburne: The Critical Heritage* (1970), an important collection of reviews of the poet's work based on Hyder's impressively researched earlier volume *Swinburne's Literary Career and Fame* (1933). *Swinburne as Critic* (1972), also edited by Hyder, gathered together hitherto out-of-print and inaccessible articles and essays by Swinburne. These works alongside a special Swinburne issue of the journal *Victorian Poetry* (1971), edited by Cecil Lang, laid the ground for critical reassessment.

In spite of general neglect, Swinburne has always had a core of loyal supporters and has tended to be lucky in those who choose to make him the subject of scholarly study; the small but steady stream of literary critical monographs produced on him throughout the last forty years of the twentieth century generally was of a high standard, most of these authored by critics working in the United States. I am thinking here of the valuable book-length studies by Thomas E. Connolly (1964), Robert L. Peters (1965), David Riede (1978), Kerry McSweeney (1981), Antony Harrison (1988), and the Canadian scholar Margot Louis (1990) written during the period 1960 to 1990, the outstanding critical work remaining *Swinburne: An Experiment in Criticism* (1972) by Jerome McGann. Newcomers to Swinburne with access to a good academic library could benefit from any one of these works as well as from shorter introductory pieces by John Rosenberg and William Buckler published in 1967 and 1980 respectively. Yet a number of these works are already out of print; others are expensive or hard to get hold of; and, as the dates suggest, there were comparatively few books written on Swinburne during the 1990s, exceptions being the fine updated biography by the British scholar Rikky Rooksby (1997) and a collection of scholarly essays co-edited by Rooksby and Nicholas Shrimpton in 1993.

Since 1990 Swinburne has, however, been the subject of various articles, essays and book chapters. Many of these pieces have read him in the light of modern thinking on issues of gender and sexuality; others review him as stylist. Two recent studies of Swinburne that try to bring together questions of style and sexuality can be found in Yopie Prins's *Victorian Sappho* (1999) and in my own *The Female Sublime from Milton to Swinburne: Bearing Blindness* (2001). Again, because of the specialist nature of periodical and academic publishing, it may not always be easy for general readers to track these pieces down, although the best of them are listed in the bibliography at the end of this book. There are, however, a number of paperback editions of Swinburne's poems currently available. In addition to L. M. Findlay's *Swinburne: Selected Poems* (1982, reissued 2002) and the 1995 reprint by Wordsworth Classics of Laurence Binyon's 1939 selection, two more recent editions are the inexpensive short selection in the Everyman's Poetry Library Series (1997), which I designed for an undergraduate or general audience, and Kenneth Haynes's excellent Penguin edition (2000) of Swinburne's *Poems and Ballads & Atalanta in Calydon*, the first complete annotated version of *Poems and Ballads* (1866). Jerome McGann and Charles Sligh's impressive new Yale University Press edition, *Swinburne: The Major Poems and Selected Prose*, scheduled to appear in late 2004, is likely to become a major resource in the future. So far then we have some useful introductory editions, but at the moment there is little in print available to general readers that might help them orient themselves in reading the poems.

This book aims to fill that gap by examining a representative sample of Swinburne's work as poet and critic. Swinburne's collected works fill twenty volumes of Edmund Gosse and Thomas Wise's unreliable Bonchurch edition of 1926, and it has been suggested that there is as much of his work unpublished as published. This study makes no claim to be other than very selective, introducing works that I consider to be of primary interest to a new reader. For this reason I have concentrated on the poetry up to 1882, for which Swinburne is most celebrated, as well as considering some of his most influential prose essays. Chapter 1 opens with a consideration of *Poems and Ballads* (1866), concentrating on issues of style and sympathy, performs close readings of two key poems, 'Before the Mirror' and 'Sapphics', and moves on to an examination of Swinburne's erotic poem 'Pasiphae', written in 1867, which remained unpublished during his lifetime and has subsequently been available only in limited press editions. (The text of this poem is printed in the Appendix.) Chapter 2 gives an overview of *Songs before Sunrise* (1871), Swinburne's volume of republican verse, and provides illustrative readings of two poems, 'Relics' and 'A Vision of Spring in Winter', from *Poems and Ballads 2* (1878), while Chapter 3 examines Swinburne as critic, focusing on three of his most influential impressionist prose essays on Baudelaire, Rossetti and Simeon Solomon. A short coda considers Swinburne's marvellous Arthurian epic *Tristram of Lyonesse* (1882), which many Swinburneians believe to be his masterpiece. Throughout it has been my practice to show how, far from being empty musical exercises, Swinburne's poems repay careful close analysis, establishing their meanings through a skilful allusive use of images and motifs, intertextual echo and a superb handling of poetic form.

Considerations of space and the introductory nature of this volume mean that omissions from this survey include Swinburne's many dramatic works and his criticism after 1871, along with other later interesting poems. The omission of verse published after 1882 should not be seen as endorsing the often-expressed opinion that Swinburne wrote no poetry of value during his Putney years. As is the case with many poets, Swinburne's imaginative powers waned during the later part of his life, although he was still capable on occasion of producing some extraordinary poems that refute charges of sterility and non-development such as 'A Nympholept' and

'The Lake of Gaube', both of which I discussed in *The Female Sublime*. The conclusion to this study lists various other later poems worth reading that interested readers will wish to explore for themselves.

1

Style and Sympathy in the Early Poetry

It is hardly an exaggeration to say that no other volume of English poetry published before or since, ever created so great a sensation as this. If Byron awoke to find himself famous the day after the first cantos of *Childe Harold* made their appearance, Mr Swinburne awoke to find himself both famous and notorious. For the *Poems and Ballads* not only showed that a new poet had arisen with a voice of his own, and possessed of an absolutely unexampled command of the resources of English rhythm, but they also showed that the author deemed fit for poetical treatment certain passional aspects of human life concerning which the best English tradition had hitherto been one of reticence. (*SCH* 208)

So wrote the American critic W. M. Payne in 1897, as he reflected on the appearance of *Poems and Ballads* in 1866, the volume that made Swinburne 'the most talked-of man in England'.[1] Certainly poets before Swinburne had tackled sexually controversial topics and had been criticized for it. In a somewhat more liberal climate reviewers had been scandalized by Byron's picaresque *Don Juan* (1818) and had been generally appalled by *The Cenci* (1819), Shelley's tragedy about rape and incest. After Victoria's accession in 1837, standards became stricter, and poetry in particular was expected to be morally uplifting and edifying. The 'passional aspects of human life' were not considered appropriate topics for poetic treatment by men or women. This did not mean that poets did not venture into this territory, for there were, of course, exceptions: Browning often struck a sexually provocative or disturbing note, and indeed his treatment of adultery in *Pippa*

13

Passes (1841) won him some censure, but, perhaps because his poetry was deemed 'obscure' and 'difficult', he tended not to attract adverse attention. Others were not so fortunate: Arthur Hugh Clough was reprimanded for indelicacy in 1849 for some innocuous poems about sexual attraction in *Ambavalia*; there were strong objections to the references to prostitution, rape and illegitimacy in *Aurora Leigh* (1856), Barrett Browning's epic of contemporary life; and, in 1861, Thackeray, as editor of the *Cornhill Magazine*, refused to publish 'Lord Walter's Wife', her treatment of the sexual double standard. The following year George Meredith's *Modern Love*, a sonnet sequence about marital infidelity and breakdown, was roundly criticized by many for – in the words of R. H. Hutton, reviewer for the *Spectator* (24 May 1862) – 'meddling causelessly and somewhat pruriently with a deep and painful subject he has no convictions to express'. It is significant that Swinburne was one of Meredith's defenders, replying to Hutton in the *Spectator* for 7 June, with the firmly expressed view that poetry should not be a repository for moral sentiment: 'There are pulpits enough for all preachers in prose; the business of verse-writing is hardly to express convictions.'[2]

In fact, with regard to prose, specifically the novel, things were rather more advanced. Although it is broadly true, as Edmund Gosse suggested, that the 1860s marked the midpoint of Victorian conservatism, it was also a time when, like Barrett Browning and Meredith, some novelists were beginning to question prevailing morals and manners. Encouraged by the example of French authors such as Balzac and Flaubert, the sensation novelists Wilkie Collins, Mary E. Braddon, Mrs Henry Wood and the slightly later Rhoda Broughton had begun to explore marriage and sexual relationships in a more critical fashion and to suggest that middle-class domestic life with its various ties and obligations might not be the idyll it was supposed to be. Sensation novels revealed how in middle- and upper-class households disquietening secrets were preserved for the sake of propriety, often at high cost to vulnerable family members, especially women. Novelists alerted readers to these secrets by having characters display criminally or morally aberrant behaviour such as bigamy, theft, murder, blackmail, fraud or deception, or by presenting extreme psychical symptoms such as obsession, madness and hysteria. Sensation novels proved immensely popular with the public in spite of the strong disapproval of the critics, who regarded them as a low-brow down-market phenomenon. Swinburne loved sensation fiction, which he read voraciously, but the transgressive nature of these novels paled into insignificance beside *Poems and Ballads*, which, in addition to poems featuring murder and adultery, contained poems about heterosexual coupling, and, even more controversially, sadomasochism, incest, necrophilia and lesbianism. Moreover, while the transgressive heroes and heroines of sensation fiction were summarily condemned or punished by their authors for their misdemeanours, there was no overt retribution or moral judgement for the characters in Swinburne's poems. In this, Swinburne parted company with those of his poetic predecessors who had tackled sexually sensitive topics, most of whose works included a recognizable ethical framework (even if this was not wholly sincere or whole-hearted), or at least encouraged or prompted readers to exercise moral judgement. Those who treated such topics tended to frame them clearly as dramatic or historical in nature, putting some safe distance between reader and poem, but also the poet and the poem. Finally most poets chose to write about such matters in styles that seemed appropriate to the subject matter; that is, they adopted attitudes, tones and language that signalled, or apologetically acknowledged, the unsavoury, grotesque or illicit nature of the topics they were treating.

In *Poems and Ballads* Swinburne contravened most of these conventions. In the first instance the poems did not appear to condemn the sexually controversial matter they described, to express a concern with moral judgement or to encourage it in the reader; indeed, they seemed to condone or even celebrate the acts and desires they described. Secondly, although Swinburne did use historical settings and employed dramatic personae as speakers, the physical treatment of the setting was often minimal or merely suggestive, while the dramatic characterization of these speakers was not always as fully realized or accentuated as it might be, say, in a monologue by Browning, thus putting less distance between reader and poem and making it easier for the reader to collapse such personae into the author. Thirdly, in line with the note of celebration, not only was there nothing apologetic about the tone and stance adopted by Swinburne, but he chose to write about dubious topics in a way that suggested he found them aesthetically interesting, beautiful or even admirable, and did so using language, metres and form more readily identified with lyricism to provocative and unsettling effect. By way of introduction, then, it seems useful to take each of these issues in turn to explore what Swinburne's opinions and practice were with regard to morality, voice and form.

To begin then with morality: his defence of Meredith being a case in point, Swinburne believed that 'a poet's business is presumably to write good verses, and by no means to redeem the age and remould society' ('Baudelaire', *SAC* 28). His adherence to the French literary principle of art for art's sake meant that for him the aesthetic appeal of a work was primary, although he never denied that a successful work of art might contain elements of a moral, philanthropic or political nature. At the same time he pitted himself against mainstream morality as he challenged the consensus about what topics were fit for literary treatment and publication. Like other writers, he resented the fact that publishers and editors would print only material that they felt would not compromise the most innocent members of the reading public – in effect infantilizing authors and readers and depriving them of the opportunity to explore adult issues. When defending Meredith, Swinburne complained of the absurdity of restricting writers to this standard; indeed, this was a subject to which he would recur in 'Notes on Poems and Reviews', his defence of *Poems and Ballads* ('our time has room only for such as are content to write for children and girls' (Haynes, 409; *SR* 24)). As the 'passional aspects of human life' were treated in classical texts commonly set for translation by public schoolboys, why should these same topics, artistically handled, be forbidden to contemporary authors and their audiences? A truly skilful artist should be able to take subjects generally felt to be repellent and disturbing and represent them in such a way as to make them not merely acceptable but attractive to contemplate, thus opening his readers' eyes to new ideas and influences. Thus, as Swinburne says of Baudelaire in his 1862

16

review of *Les Fleurs du mal*, 'even of the loathsomest bodily putrescence and decay, he can make some noble use; pluck out its meaning and secret, even its beauty in a certain way, from actual carrion' (*SAC* 30). Swinburne does not indicate to his readers the moral position he expects them to adopt; instead, he emphasizes other qualities while simultaneously expecting them to expand their sense of what morality and representation can and should be.

With regard to voice, we might well wonder how readers interpreted Swinburne's use of this in *Poems and Ballads*, where dramatic speakers such as the clerk in 'The Leper' and Sappho in 'Anactoria' are ranged side by side with a large number of unspecified speakers and anonymous voices who give poetic expression to a variety of different perspectives or emotions. At a time when sincerity was prized and use of the dramatic monologue was itself still not perfectly understood, readers may well have been confused by the distinctions between Swinburne's different poems and, ignoring substantial differences in tone, fallen into indiscriminately regarding all the poems as thinly masked expressions of their author's experiences and opinions. Moreover, the lack of actual dramatic action in some of the monologues might help persuade a reader, for example, that Sappho in 'Anactoria' is merely the mouthpiece of Swinburne, particularly when her more personal discussion of conflicted sexual feelings gives way to a long philosophical meditation on time, transience and immortality. A lack of specificity in a generic character such as the Roman speaker of the 'Hymn to Proserpine', the 'Last Pagan' as Swinburne called him (*Letters*, i. 11), may have helped make his anti-Christian views seem recuperable as those of his author. The more anonymous voices that narrate poems such as 'An Interlude', 'The Garden of Proserpine' or 'Satia te Sanguine' can thus all the more easily be seen as those of the poet himself. It is this failure of readerly discrimination that Swinburne deplores in his critical defence 'Notes on Poems and Reviews' (1866) when he protests that his poems were 'dramatic, many-faced, multifarious; and no utterance of enjoyment or despair, belief or unbelief, can properly be assumed as the assertion of its author's personal feeling or faith' (Haynes, 404; *SR* 18). This protest, however, does not deny that the collection contains personal or autobiographical material, and indeed, in the much later 'Dedicatory Epistle' with which he prefaced the 1904 edition of his *Collected Poetical Works*, Swinburne admitted more freely:

> there are photographs from life in the book; and there are sketches from imagination. Some which keen-sighted criticism has dismissed with a smile as ideal or imaginary were as real and actual as they well could be: others which have been taken as obvious transcripts from memory were utterly fantastic or dramatic. If the two kinds cannot be distinguished, it is surely rather a credit than a discredit to an artist whose medium or material has more in common with a musician's than with a sculptor's. (*PS* i, p. vii; *SR* 92)

Obviously it was annoying for Swinburne, having experimented with a variety of different kinds of address, to have them all passed off as confessional autobiography or transparent opinion. This was plainly not the result he desired. The apparent lack of distinction between the different kinds of verse did not represent an attempt to foist his autobiographical self on readers but, as the final sentence quoted above implies, instead resulted from an artistic impulse to work over and transform personal material and amalgamate it with other categories. What, then, on a simple reading might appear to close the gap between poem and poet could on deeper consideration be an extended exploration of the notion of poetic persona or identity. In subduing or toning down specific localized detail and juxtaposing dramatic with autobiographical poems, the dramatic becomes apparently more 'personal', but, by the same token, in artistically abstracting, refining and transforming the voice of personal experience and setting it alongside dramatic performances, personal experience becomes more 'dramatic' and generic and less individual and circumstantial. The total effect is to make the personal 'impersonal'; that is to say, aesthetically transformed subjectivity becomes not an expression of the writer's personality or his quotidian self, but the artistic persona or symbolic identity he adopts in his poems. Although there are a number of places where Swinburne's verse is clearly spoken by an identifiable character, and although the verse is spoken from a variety of

18

situations and occasions, we tend to encounter less a series of fully characterized individual speakers than the genetically related manifestations of a flexible poetic persona who can adopt a variety of different positions and perspectives. Naive readers may have associated this persona with the poet's own private biographical self, but we should not assume that all Swinburne's Victorian readers read him naively. When Marie Corelli in her guise of 'The Silver Domino' comments on Swinburne's epic *Tristram of Lyonesse* (1882), she shows how another kind of reading takes strength from impersonality:

> In perusing its pages, one scarcely thinks of the author save as the merest human phonograph through which Inspiration speaks – in fact, it is rather curious to realise how little we really do take the personal Swinburne into our consideration while reading his works, or for that matter the personal anybody who has done anything.[3]

Indeed, as Maud Ellman implies, one of the reasons that T. S. Eliot may have been so ready to sideline Swinburne in 1920 was that he was made uncomfortable by the fact that his precursor had already put into practice the theory of impersonality described by him in 'Tradition and the Individual Talent' in 1919.[4]

The fact that a substantially large number of the speakers of *Poems and Ballads* are not overdetermined allows readers to try on or inhabit temporarily the subjective and emotional states described. A poem such as the notorious 'Dolores', addressed to 'the darker Venus', also unsettles by its use of the first-person plural, a device that breaks down distance, allying potentially complicit readers with the speaker. It is easy to see why such a poem with its satisfyingly regular rhythms and strong rhetorical patterns was immediately taken up as an anthem by groups of Oxford undergraduates:

> And pale from the past we draw nigh thee,
> And satiate with comfortless hours;
> And we know thee, how all men belie thee,
> And we gather the fruit of thy flowers . . .

> (Haynes, 127)

19

SYMPATHY AND SADOMASOCHISM

This example of inclusiveness leads us into matters of form and style. Swinburne's poetry tends to encourage the reader not to assent to moral or didactic propositions but to draw him or her into sympathy with the aesthetic and emotional atmosphere of the verse. It is in this atmosphere that the poem communicates its ideas, often less through overt argument than through its images and metre and rhythms. Rhythm and metre in themselves naturally help dramatize the symbolic meaning of the verse, but Yeats's proposition that 'the purpose of rhythm ... is to prolong the moment of contemplation ... to keep us in that state of perhaps real trance in which the mind liberated from the pressure of the will is unfolded in symbols' is a good description of the way in which Swinburne's often mesmerizing metres can lull readers into acquiescence so that they absorb through the poem's imagery controversial or disturbing ideas they might otherwise not tolerate.[5] In Swinburne's, as in all good poetry, form is an integral part of the meaning or argument and not a cosmetic afterthought, something added to 'dress up' ideas and content. For him, moreover, form vitalizes ordinary language, creating meaning and argument, and giving this renewed language unexpected energy and attack. In his unfinished novel *Lesbia Brandon*, one of Swinburne's lead female characters, Lady Wariston, voices to one of her young sons views that sound remarkably like those of her author:

> Things in verse hurt one, don't they? hit and sting like a cut. They wouldn't hurt us if we had no blood, and no nerves. Verse hurts horribly: people have died of verse-making, and thought their mistresses killed them – or their reviewers. You have the nerve of poetry – the soft place it hits on, and stings. Never write verse when you get big; people who do are bad, or mad, or sick. ... It's odd that words should change so just by being put into rhyme. They get teeth and bite; they take fire and burn. I wonder who first thought of tying words up and twisting them back to make verses, and hurt and delight all the people in the world for ever. For one can't do without it now: we like it far too much, I suspect, you and I. It was an odd device: one can't see why this ringing and rhyming of words should make all the difference in them: one can't tell where the pain or the pleasure ends or begins. (*LB* 148)

20

Swinburne's readers are meant to experience themselves as physical as well as intellectual beings as the verse communicates simultaneously to the mind and senses, predominantly through that psychologically charged bodily element: the nerves. An analogous phrase much beloved by Swinburne, which he found in Shakespeare and used often in his own poetry and prose, was 'the spirit of sense'. This epithet, which nicely conveys the mergence of mental and sensuous faculties, has special reference to the nerves, for, in Elizabethan physiology, the spirits of the senses 'were subtle vapors, transmitted through the nerves (thought of as hollow tubes), and believed to be the intermediaries between man's body and soul'.[6] Lady Wariston's son has a susceptibility to verse, 'the nerve of poetry – the soft place it hits on, and stings', whereas elsewhere, in an essay on 'Dante Gabriel Rossetti', Swinburne describes how a poem, 'Penumbra', displays its author's 'mastery of hand': 'the finest nerves of life are finely touched; the quiver and ache of soul and senses to which all things are kindled and discoloured by half morbid lights of emotion give a burning pulse of melody to the verses' (*ES* 70). Evidently such passages are informed – in the first instance explicitly, in the second implicitly – by Swinburne's own sadomasochism, not terribly interesting in a limited biographical sense, but of great interest when seen as shaping his philosophy and aesthetics. Thus with regard to literary creativity Swinburne sees the transmutative activity of form as a liberating violence, binding and disciplining language and yet also releasing its energy. Form gives language its teeth so that the finished poem is itself a pleasurable violence exerted on the sensibility of the reader.

Such seemingly idiosyncratic views should not blind us to the fact that complex relations between pain and pleasure are well-attested constituents of other major aesthetic experiences such as the sublime, which, according to Edmund Burke, is a shock to the mind and senses accompanied by sensations of awe, wonder or surprise, and is induced by intimations of pain and danger. The earlier classical version of the sublime attributed to Longinus seems primarily stylistic and literary, but attains a more emotional physicalized character in its sympathetic depiction of Sappho's love-torment, setting up

21

potential for an understanding of the sublime as a scene of sympathy and identification with emotional excess, usually generated by another's pain or suffering. In both these versions of the sublime emotional and other mental responses cannot easily be separated from physicality. Both involve relations of dominance and submission, as the witness of sublimity becomes temporarily subject to, possessed or mastered by the spectacle or phenomenon he experiences. That Swinburne's poetry frequently draws on the sublime in terms of both style and subject matter is hardly surprising when we see how it complements his own sense of what poetry is and should do to a reader. His insistence that poetry remind readers that they have bodies as well as minds and that the two cannot be separated, a reminder that comes as much through form as it does through the many images of bodies that occupy the poems, also finds expression in his characteristic use of synaesthesia or mixing of sense-impressions found in both his poetry and his prose; Blake's verses, for example, he famously described as having 'a fragrance of sound, a melody of colour' (*WB* 9; *SB* 233). Synaesthesia, a form of hyper-sensory stimulation, which temporarily unsettles both mental and physical perception, again breaks down boundaries in a manner that is both potentially pleasurable and disturbing, exposing the subject to new ideas and sensations. Such an experience might well be intoxicating. As Lady Wariston suggests, readers and writers who find themselves susceptible to the exquisite and subtle pains of poetry become addicted, find themselves with a poetic habit: 'For one can't do without it now: we like it far too much, I suspect, you and I.' She also advises her son, 'Never write verse when you get big; people who do are bad, or mad, or sick', the implication being that those who possess poetic sensibility, 'the nerve of poetry', risk growing into full-blown 'sick' poets – the sensitive poet of the Romantics becoming, in Swinburne's jokey logic, the 'pervert' in thrall to the inherently sadomasochistic practice of poetry.

Typically in sadomasochistic practices pain and pleasure become hard to separate – 'one can't tell where the pain or the pleasure ends or begins' – as boundaries merge and fuse. We have seen this pattern emerge elsewhere in Swinburne as he closes the gap or complicates the distinctions between mind and body, personal and dramatic. He was naturally drawn to what he called 'the identity of contraries . . . the latent relations of pain and pleasure, the subtle conspiracies of good with evil, the deep alliances of death and life, of love and hate, of attraction and abhorrence' (SS 455) and his love of fusing antitheses or contraries and his interest in transitions and the brief interspaces that occur at boundaries have been well documented.[7] This boundary blurring and subsequent diffi-culty in distinguishing one thing from its opposite becomes part of the experience of reading Swinburne. It was to an instance of this boundary blurring that the *fin-de-siècle* social commentator Max Nordau objected when he included Swin-burne among the artists he attacked in his study *Degeneration* (1895), where he singled out as an example of degenerate style, not one of Swinburne's more overtly provocative poems, but the ballad 'The King's Daughter'. Nordau took issue not with the poem's cryptic subject matter – an apparently incestuous relationship between one of the king's daughters and her brother – but the way in which the poem narrates the story through associated natural images. While he claimed to find permissible the use of pathetic fallacy – the projection of the subject's moods onto inanimate nature – he objected to Swinburne's use of nature in the poem:

> He does not let the external world express a mood, but makes it tell a story; he changes its appearance according to the character of the events he is describing. Like an orchestra, it accompanies all events which are somewhere taking place. Here nature is no longer a white wall on which, as in a game of shadows, the varied visions of the soul are thrown; but a living, thinking being, which follows the sinful love-romance with the same tense sympathy as the poet, and which, with its own media, expresses just as much as he does – complacency, delight, or sorrow – at every chapter of the story.[8]

Arguably what Swinburne is doing is not essentially very different from the pathetic fallacy that can both be chameleonic and have a narrative function; moreover, what Nordau intends by 'the poet' is unclear and perhaps naive. Nonetheless the description of Swinburne's attempt to make nature into a commentator who sympathetically expresses his views implies the breaking of a boundary and the extension of consciousness.

This seems analogous to the process that can happen to the reader of Swinburne's poetry

Swinburne's poetry is evidently intended to break down readers' boundaries, not just in terms of their taboos and prejudices, but also by making a concerted effort to get into their space, to occupy or take up a place in their consciousness. As we noticed in Lady Wariston's speech, Swinburne invests poetic language with a surprisingly active agency – it assaults the reader – and certainly this seems to correspond to the ways in which his verse represents itself and is commonly represented, as it makes a concerted bid to penetrate, ensnare, win over, charm or seduce the witting or unwitting reader. At the same time it lays itself out as an object to be consumed, absorbed or internalized, its metres, rhythms and verbal fluency naturally lending themselves to memorization and recitation, so that Swinburne's words, taken into the reader's consciousness, are then embodied, reproduced through the materiality of speech as the speaker's own. Because of the way Swinburne's verse has particular designs on the sensibility of readers, their bodies and minds, there can arise a sense that they are not quite sure what belongs to the poem and what to themselves, a sense of not being quite sure of where their identities and those of the poems begin and end. Swinburne brilliantly described this seduction and domination of the reader by textual power in an essay of 1871 on the poetry of the Caroline playwright John Ford:

> No poet is less forgetable [*sic*] than Ford; none fastens (as it were) the fangs of his genius and his will more deeply in your memory. You cannot shake hands with him and pass by; you cannot fall in with him and out again at pleasure; if he touch you once he takes you, and what he takes he keeps his hold of; his work becomes part of your thought and part of your spiritual furniture for ever; he signs himself upon you as with a seal of deliberate and decisive power. (*ES* 312–13)

Ford's poetry, metonymically represented by 'Ford', an aggressive sexually dominant personality, takes ineradicable possession of the susceptible reader. What Swinburne admires in other writers is frequently an index to his own literary characteristics, and, while a tendency to annex readerly identity may be true of much literature, it seems particularly so of

24

Swinburne because of the way his verse blurs and compromises boundaries.

This pattern of making what properly or seemingly belongs to one entity belong to another, of transplanting one party's feelings and sensations into another's breast, looks like an enforced or manipulated parodic version of sympathy. As inheritors of eighteenth-century and Romantic ideals of sensibility, Victorian writers and critics were keen to promote ideals of sympathy, advocating the benefits that can occur when one individual enters into and shares another's feelings. Sympathy was commonly held as a means of encouraging the growth of moral sentiment and ennobling human nature, and art and literature could help in this process by enabling viewers and readers to identify with others. In George Eliot's formulation: 'Art is the nearest thing to life; it is a mode of amplifying experience and extending our contact with our fellow-men beyond the bounds of our personal lot.' Sympathy was thus seen as strengthening society by the encouragement of socially cohesive bonds between different groups, and for that reason middle-class novelists in particular saw it as a way of educating their readers about the lower classes and the difficulties faced by those with less privileged lives. Thus Eliot's narrator declares in *Adam Bede* (1859): 'In this world there are so many ... common, coarse people, who have no sentimental wretchedness! It is so needful we should remember their existence ... Therefore let Art always remind us of them.'[9] However, as this last example makes clear, this kind of sympathy and the model of society it supports is essentially conservative, identifying and explaining the artisan or 'vulgar citizen' to the middle-class reader without questioning the social *status quo* – 'let Art always remind *us* of *them*'. One might argue that this kind of sympathy even as it appears to cross boundaries serves merely to reinforce them. Moreover, as one reads Victorian fiction, it becomes evident that various groups or individuals, in particular those that threaten social or domestic order such as striking workers or sexually transgressive women, are deemed far less deserving of sympathy than others, and that narrators can be intrusively directive about whom and what readers should feel sympathy for. Some feelings and situations are to be sympathized with while others are evidently beyond the pale. Indeed, narrators themselves in withholding sympathy for certain characters and situations can seem judgemental and punitive. This kind of sympathy, evidently carefully controlled and administered, makes us aware of the latent sadism that often underlies the sympathetic philanthropic impulse.

In contrast to the mainstream conventions of sympathy there were, of course, other expressions that did not corroborate approved moral sentiment. These expressions of sympathy would not have been recognized as such, even though they partake of the mechanism of crossing boundaries and transplanting feeling. Instead they would have been seen as dangerous in that they ask readers to entertain thoughts and feelings deemed 'unhealthy' that should properly be contained or repressed. Here the boundary crossing of sympathy could have a degenerative or polluting effect in that ideas and emotions deemed to damage social and moral fibre might spread and harm the larger community. Damaging ideas and emotions might include radical political, religious or social views, challenges to established morality especially in the area of sexuality, and the overt expression of sexual feeling itself. Sexual feeling was deemed to be particularly contaminating and the controlling standard of what was thought permissible in print was governed by the figure of the sexually innocent young girl. But sexual feelings are among the most easily roused, and pornography or erotic literature and art has the potential, if not always the capability, to arouse sympathetic identification. Swinburne's verse evidently encourages sexual sympathy, not just in terms of exposing readers to potentially arousing material, but in making them think about the mutable nature of desire and the different forms it can take. While sexuality is an evident area in which to engage and challenge readerly sympathy, Swinburne's libertarian politics and free-thinking attitudes make similar appeals. One of the major characteristics of his poetry is the way in which he persuades his readers to entertain or give mental space to ideas and feelings with which they would normally not be in sympathy by bringing them into proximity with characters and situations they would habitually shun. This is something I shall examine in the rest of this chapter.

POEMS AND BALLADS (1866)

The predominant theme of *Poems and Ballads* is love; not the conventional romantic love of Victorian heterosexual courtship and marriage, but love as 'bittersweet' to use the famous characterization coined by Sappho (Fragment 130), the classical woman poet Swinburne believed to be 'simply nothing less than the greatest poet who ever was at all' (*Letters*, iv. 124). It is also intimately informed, as Antony Harrison has shown, by the medieval courtly-love tradition, a tradition that we might say is inherently masochistic, in which the male troubadour abases himself before the unattainable lady of his affections, and sings of 'a passion which can never be requited in this world, of death as preferable to any human reward and of the duty of separation from the beloved'.[10] The identification of the beloved woman with a man's ideals, values and aspirations and the theme of escape from the suffering of love into death are other courtly-love motifs shown by Harrison to be carried through into Swinburne's poetry.

Along with love, time and transience are keynotes in *Poems and Ballads* that echo in a substantial number of the volume's sixty-two poems. The most famous poems examine obsessive sexual desire or feature the *femme fatale*. 'Laus Veneris', 'Phædra', 'Anactoria', 'The Triumph of Time', 'Les Noyades', 'The Leper' and 'Satia te Sanguine' explore the psychology of sexual obsession and, in particular, the cruelty of love, while 'Faustine' and 'Dolores' are the best-known poems that feature the *femme fatale*. Both are deliberately excessive histrionic poems that apparently eulogize exotic, sexually voracious female figures as antidotes to the Victorian Angel in the House and endorse sexual experience and experimentation over contemporary ideals of chastity and marital fidelity. (Yet this celebration is not unequivocal, even if one does not agree with Watts's description of 'Dolores' as 'a wail from the bed of vice – a Jeremiad on the misery of pleasure'.[11]) The *femme fatale* recurs in the mythologized figure of Lucrezia Borgia in 'A Ballad of Life' and 'A Ballad of Death', as Venus in 'Laus Veneris', as the sexually ambiguous being in 'Fragoletta', as the allegorical biblical whore in the eponymous 'Aholibah', and as various of the women who process through 'The Masque of

27

Queen Bersabe'. Other poems explore sexual disappointment. As Lawrence Lipking has explained in his study *Abandoned Women and Poetic Tradition* (1988), it is comparatively rare to find poems written in the voice of the abandoned male lover.[12] Swinburne is unusual in this in that some of his key poems voice the anger, pain or resentment of the male lover who has been ignored or spurned by his female beloved. These include 'The Triumph of Time', 'Les Noyades', 'Satia te Sanguine' and 'A Leave-Taking'. The first three of these poems also express a death wish for both the beloved and the speaker himself. Something of the bitterness of thwarted love, though expressed in a more detached and distanced way, sounds in 'Stage Love', which charts a woman's experience of a relationship that ends in cruel disappointment. A more meditative and tender note can be heard in the wistful and reflective rondels 'These many years' and 'Kissing her hair' and in 'Hesperia', a poem that is a self-acknowledged reaction against the narcotic sensuality of 'Dolores'. Other poems serenely and philosophically treat love as a temporary experience or chart the end of love affairs as inevitable: 'Rococo', 'Erotion', 'Before Dawn', 'Before Parting', 'Félise', 'Love at Sea', 'An Interlude', 'The Year of Love'. That love can be enjoyed as a fleeting pleasure is one of the chief claims of *Poems and Ballads* and one that challenged fondly held ideals of commitment and enduring love. This theme of the passing of love merges into the larger Swinburneian theme of the transience of all things. A smaller number of poems depict the lover as he or she actually enjoys the state of love: 'In the Orchard', 'Love and Sleep' and the more reticent 'August' explore the pleasure of sexual love, 'A Match' is a rare exercise in mutuality, while 'The Sundew' and the courtly 'Madonna Mia' pay homage in different ways to the beloved woman.

Although the larger part of the poems in *Poems and Ballads* treat sexual love and desire, it would be wrong to assume this is the only topic addressed. Swinburne's dissatisfaction with orthodox Christianity and Theism is explored most famously in his 'Hymn to Proserpine', but also in 'Anactoria' and 'A Litany'. The theme of general transience and change is addressed in 'Anima Anceps' and 'A Ballad of Burdens', 'A Lamentation' and the autumnal 'Hendecasyllabics'. Death as end to or a respite from the changes and chances of life is explored in the 'pagan' sentiment of 'The Garden of Proserpine' and 'Ilicet'. Two political poems, 'A Song in Time of Order. 1852' and 'A Song in Time of Revolution. 1860', are early indications of the republican views Swinburne would express in his later *Songs before Sunrise* (1871). A large number of poems show Swinburne's interest in art and poetry and in the inspiring works of other artists and poets. Three poems directly allude to art works: 'A Christmas Carol' to the watercolour of the same name by D. G. Rossetti; 'Before the Mirror' to Whistler's painting *The Little White Girl*, later known as *Symphony in White No. 2*; and 'Hermaphroditus' to the antique hermaphrodite statue in the Louvre. 'Erotion', as Swinburne later explained in an essay on his friend, the painter Simeon Solomon, was a 'comment' on Solomon's *Damon and Aglae*. There are three poems addressed to illustrious contemporaries: an elegy for the recently deceased poet Walter Savage Landor, whom Swinburne had visited in Italy in 1864 and the dedicatee of his classical drama *Atalanta in Calydon*, a paean to Swinburne's hero, the poet, dramatist and novelist Victor Hugo, and 'Dedication. 1865' addressed to Swinburne's friend, the painter Edward Burne-Jones, the dedicatee of *Poems and Ballads*. Other poems show Swinburne's intimate knowledge of poetic tradition as he indirectly honours poets from a range of periods and nationalities by imitating their forms and narratives: 'At Eleusis' follows the *Homeric Hymn to Demeter* in which the goddess Demeter tells the story of her time after the loss of her daughter Persephone when she became nurse to Triptolemus, son of Celeus and Metaneira and tried to make him immortal; 'Sapphics' honours Sappho and uses her characteristic metre, and 'Hendecasyllabics' uses the characteristic meter of Catullus. 'April' is a translation of a poem by the medieval poet Guillaume de Ferrières, Vidame de Chartres, 'The Two Dreams' is an adaptation of a love story from Boccaccio's *Decameron*, while 'St Dorothy' imitates Chaucer's style and idiom. 'Love at Sea' is a free translation of Théophile Gautier's 'Barcarolle', while 'Hermaphroditus' indirectly honours Gautier's poem 'Contralto', also inspired by the Louvre sculpture. Mischievously included by Swinburne without reference to its original author, 'Song before Death' is a translation of an innocuous song by the less-than-innocuous Marquis de Sade, while 'A Ballad of Burdens' adopts the French *ballade* form used by another of Swinburne's favourite poets, François Villon.

In addition to the French *ballade*, the volume is notable for its ambitious coverage of fixed poetic forms: the Italian *canzone* used in 'A Ballad of Life' and 'A Ballad of Death', the Provençal *alba* or dawn-song used in 'In the Orchard', the French *rondeau* that gives rise to the two poems called 'Rondel', while the north-country ballad, a form much beloved by Swinburne, inspired 'The King's Daughter', 'After Death', 'May Janet', 'The Bloody Son' and 'The Sea-Swallows'. Swinburne also showed his proficiency in the sonnet form in 'Hermaphroditus', 'A Cameo' and 'Love and Sleep', and produced fine pastiches of the medieval carol in 'A Christmas Carol', the medieval miracle-drama in 'The Masque of Queen Bersabe', and classical Greek drama in the fragment 'Phædra'. His love of imitation also surfaces in other poems: 'Laus Veneris' and 'The Leper' purport to be inspired by medieval sources that are 'cited' as epigraphs or subscriptions, but that were in fact masterfully fabricated by the poet himself. His perceptive ear allowed him to produce a range of poems that convincingly mimic the language and tones of biblical, classical and medieval literature. However, the astonishing formal versatility of *Poems and Ballads* may actually have been held against the poet to fuel the prejudice that his poetry is all sound and no sense, and this in spite of Swinburne's remonstrations in his essay on Dante Gabriel Rossetti:

> It is said sometimes that a man may have a strong and perfect style who has nothing to convey worth conveyance under it. This is indeed a favourite saying of men who have no words in which to convey the thoughts they have not ... But it remains for them to prove as well as assert that beauty and power of expression can accord with emptiness or sterility of matter, or that impotence of articulation must imply depth and wealth of thought. (*ES* 63)

The two poems I have chosen from *Poems and Ballads* – 'Before the Mirror' and 'Sapphics' – show how Swinburne's verse repays attentive close reading, for both have complex and interesting things to say that could easily be overlooked by readers who see them merely as stylistic exercises. Both poems also stage some of the wider issues and principles at stake in the volume, with the second poem, 'Sapphics', becoming a sort of poetic manifesto. They are followed by a reading of 'Pasiphae', a considerably less-well-known Swinburne poem, written probably at about the same time as *Poems and Ballads* or a little later, which would have been too controversial to publish in Swinburne's lifetime. In 1869 Swinburne's poetry, like Tennyson's, would be famously deprecated as 'feminine' for its concentration on love and female figures by the critic Alfred Austin, who nonetheless observed that, while Tennyson's treatment of femininity was 'proper', Swinburne's was 'improper' (*SCH* 105). Illustrating Swinburne's tendency to identify with female figures, and, in particular, women deemed 'improper', all three poems selected centre on the figure of a woman at odds with conventional sexual morality.

I start with 'Before the Mirror' (Haynes, 103–5), which bears the subscriptions '(Verses written under a Picture)' and 'Inscribed to J. A. Whistler'. Swinburne wrote this poem to accompany the picture by James McNeill Whistler called 'The Little White Girl' (now in the Tate Britain, London), after viewing it in the painter's studio. The painting depicts not a little girl but a young woman dressed in white and holding a decorative fan, who, leaning on a mantelpiece over which hangs a mirror, gazes wistfully to the side. Her face is reflected, although her gaze does not actually seem to coincide with that of her mirror image. What is also interesting is that there seems to be a discrepancy between the face of the young woman and the face of her reflection, which looks older and more careworn. Pink-blossomed sprays of a flowering plant, most likely an azalea, occupy the right-hand corner of the painting and can also be seen breaking into the picture just above the mantelpiece. The model for the painting was Whistler's mistress Joanna Hiffernan and the painting was displayed at the Royal Academy in 1865 with the poem printed on gold paper and pasted onto its original frame.[13] The fourth and sixth stanzas of the poem were printed in the *Royal Academy Catalogue* for 1865. 'I know it was entirely and only suggested to me by the picture,' wrote Swinburne to Whistler (*Letters*, i. 118–19) when he sent him the first six verses of the poem on 2 April 1865.[14] Yet, like 'Hermaphroditus', another poem in

Poems and Ballads inspired by an art object, the poem is no easy transcription of the picture. In contrast to Whistler's young woman, Swinburne's subject directly beholds herself in the mirror, and the poet selectively fastens on a few details – the rather wistful air of the picture, the theme of 'whiteness' and the flowers – which he then adjusts to suit his own purposes; the flowers, for example, become identified with roses and are transposed into a complex floral imagery. When the painting was shown again at the International Exhibition at the South Kensington Museum in 1872, the reviewer for *The Times* (14 May 1872) found Swinburne's 'very beautiful but not very lucid verses' unhelpful as to the painting's meaning, commenting 'Nevertheless, the picture is one . . . that means more than it says, though not so much perhaps as the poet has said for it' – a somewhat equivocal tribute that manages to suggest that the poem says both too little and too much. Whistler thought the poem superior to his painting and was warm in its praise. At the time of its composition he had endured various critical attacks and he appreciated the poet's support. As late as 1902, long after he and Swinburne had ended their friendship, he recalled the poem as 'a rare and graceful tribute from the poet to the painter – a noble recognition of work by the production of a nobler one' (Gosse, *Life*, 273).

This poem could easily be viewed as a graceful exercise in aestheticism, which plays loosely with the images of Whistler's painting in a lightly evocative manner. Whistler himself was strongly against the tendency in art criticism to read paintings as narratives, and later deliberately gave his pictures musical titles – *The Little White Girl* became *Symphony in White No. 2* – to emphasize their predominantly formal qualities. We might assume that Swinburne's poem is also an early impressionist study in the art-for-art's-sake vein. And yet I think there are more interesting ways of reading the poem. Whistler, in spite of his strategic insistence that his paintings were simply tone-and-colour studies, undoubtedly manipulated symbolic details in his paintings to hint at disturbing ambiguities. Swinburne, too, is adept at symbolism and, like *The Times* reviewer, we get the sense of both the poem's difference from the painting and its hidden plenitude of meanings.

One of the things that are odd about this poem is that it employs figures and metaphors that become curiously literalized or rather are fused with the realities they name, so that the 'narrative' of the poem proceeds both at a figurative and a literal level. Employing the standard Victorian trope, one might even call it a cliché, of the young woman as flower, the poem starts by comparing the girl to a white rose and to snowdrops. These flowers are themselves compared to or with other entities: the white rose set alongside its red compeers in a rose garden, the snowdrops blown by the cold East wind likened to timorous maidens. Such floral tributes usually betoken a young woman's inexperience, her freshness and purity, which uncomplicatedly reveal themselves in her un-blemished virginal appearance. But in Swinburne's poem the analogy is not just a stock poetic compliment, although it might easily be passed over as such. Seemingly interrogating the title of Whistler's painting and its white-clad subject, the speaker concludes that the girl is 'whiter' than both flowers, but in what does her whiteness consist and what does it signify? The last line of the stanza suggests it is triggered more by the luminous intensity of her gaze or expression than by her virtue. Swinburne seems to be flirting artfully with the language and imagery normally associated with that sanctified Victorian figure of innocence beloved by critics and publishers, the young girl. This language is applied to the young woman but in such a way that it no longer seems to hold its conventional values, implying that, in contrast to the maidenly snowdrops, the girl in Swinburne's poem is no fragile or vulnerable maiden.

The next stanza takes this hint further. It lures us in with its opening description of something that is concealed, and its teasing syntax allows for a number of possible readings to obscure perception before we find out (or think we find out) just what is 'Behind the veil, forbidden, / Shut up from sight'. Gradually revealing the subject, Swinburne's speaker ques-tions an ambiguous figure he calls 'Love'. Necessarily capital-ized because it opens the line, the word seemingly refers to the abstract personification of love. If this is the case, then the stanza interrogates the nature of sexual love, a topic that is taboo – 'Behind the veil, forbidden, / Shut up from sight' – for polite Victorian society and especially the young woman, whose curiosity may be represented in the speaker's eager enquiries. Contrasting with Victorian ideals of marital love, sexual love, identified with the 'White rose of weary leaf / 'Late rose whose life is brief, whose loves are light,' is seen as fleeting and transitory rather than stable and enduring. However, this controversial assertion may cover a cryptic and even more provocative reading in which 'Love' is a term of endearment. In this reading it is the young woman whom the speaker questions, addressing *her* as 'White rose of weary leaf, / Late rose whose life is brief, whose loves are light'. Again the floral references unsettle and a tension appears. If it is the girl who is 'Behind the veil, forbidden, / Shut up from sight', does her confinement allude to the Victorian middle-class ideology of separate spheres for men and women, with women restricted to the protective environment of the home while men venture out into the marketplace to test their abilities or earn a living? Is the girl, like a fragile flower, protected in her feminine sphere from the harsh realities of the world outside? And, if so, how does this square with the last two lines of the stanza, which seem to describe her as a mature bloom and intimate that she is no stranger to amatory experience: 'Late rose whose life is brief, whose loves are light'? 'Light' could just mean 'carefree' or 'light-hearted' or 'not serious', but 'light' in Victorian parlance, as in the phrase 'a light woman', implies sexual promiscuity. Here the white rose is not quite the flower one might have initially assumed it was in the opening stanza. Indeed, the wording of the second stanza begins to look a little curious: could one be 'forbidden, shut up from sight' for reasons other than protection, because, like sexual love itself, one was considered 'forbidden' to polite society, not fit for public display? Could the girl be a mistress or 'kept woman', like Whistler's model, or a courtesan or prostitute? Or could she be a just-married woman with 'a past' who is now enclosed in the domestic sphere? Swinburne's adaptation of certain aspects of the picture helps multiply imaginative possibilities. In Whistler's painting the white-frocked young woman wears a prominently displayed wedding ring, so that the seeming disjunction between the fresh-faced newly-wed young woman and her older, sadder image in the mirror could intimate something about the expectations and disillusionments of marriage. However, Whistler uses Jo, his 'unrespectable' mistress, to represent the respectable middle-class woman, and in so doing suggests, contrary to Victorian belief and prejudice, that 'pure' and 'impure' women may be indistinguishable. Swinburne's unsettling treatment of the Victorian language of purity may be doing the same thing. In this he shares some ground with his friends Christina and Dante Gabriel Rossetti, who both published major poems that in different ways asserted a common identity or likeness between pure and impure women. However, unlike Christina Rossetti's *Goblin Market* (1862) and Dante Gabriel Rossetti's 'Jenny' (1870), Swinburne's poem is not concerned with moral issues of rescue or redemption. In presenting his readers with an apparently familiar or merely decorative 'innocent' image that then subtly metamorphoses into something more problematic, Swinburne beguiles his readers into a sympathetic relation with a woman they would normally shun, to the point where they will share in the woman's own thoughts stirred by her image in the glass.

The last stanza of this section ends nonetheless with a faintly admonitory note of warning. Conventionally floral images are often attended by warnings that blossom time is of short duration, as in Herrick's 'Gather ye rose-buds while ye may' ('To Virgins, to Make Much of Time'). Here the images that help make the analogues of the first stanza – the garden, the hard East wind that chilled the snowdrops – are reinvoked as shadowy realities, but it now seems to be winter and the garden is empty of flowers, which disappeared 'long since' at the end of summer. What is this garden? Possibly it could be regarded as a version of the maiden's bower, traditionally a secluded room or enclosed garden retreat in which the young woman, cut off from the outside world, is left to reflect on her thoughts or emotions, which often run on the theme of love. In Victorian poetry the bower often comes to double for the protected feminine domestic sphere, although in some earlier incarnations, Spenser, for example, the bower is a place of feasting and lovemaking. But the garden or bower in Swinburne's poem, which at one time was a place of feasting and summertime warmth, now seems to be denuded of its pleasures. Now long after 'men' have left the feast,

35

the woman remains alone, threatened by the biting cold of frozen snowflakes. Whether she is a fallen woman who, now isolated or perhaps deserted, is facing the harsh chill of social disapproval or whether she has left behind a former life of pleasure for the cold comforts and confinement of matrimony, this is a woman who is 'before the mirror' at a moment of apparent crisis.

The second section of the poem gives us her voice and her thoughts, roused by her contemplation of her reflection in the mirror. But, if the concluding stanza of the previous section suggests that this might be a moment of moral insight, the woman immediately sounds defiant: ' "Come snow, come wind or thunder / High up in air, I watch my face and wonder / At my bright hair." ' Refusing to take alarm and in contrast to Whistler's woman, she finds pleasure in the fact that her reflection exhibits only a self-delighting beauty. Angela Leighton has suggested that nineteenth-century poems by women that employ the image of mirror signal the split between the woman and her reflection, where the reflection represents another, often secret self or gives access to the woman's innermost private thoughts.[15] Quite often in these poems – such as Augusta Webster's 'By the Looking Glass' (1866) and 'Faded' (written 1870, published 1893), or Mary Elizabeth Coleridge's 'The Other Side of a Mirror' (1896) – the reflected image is ugly, unflattering or in some way distressing, illuminating the woman's fears, anxieties or repressed fantasies. Such poems find a parallel in Whistler's painting. A seeming exception is Webster's 'A Castaway' (1870), in which a prostitute, scornful of yet harried by society's negative images of fallen women, looks into the mirror and finds herself 'No fiend, no slimy thing out of the pools ... A woman none dare call not beautiful, / Not womanly in every woman's grace.' But, though gratified by her reflection, Webster's speaker continues to be exercised by the competing selves she finds in her past and present lives and in popular misconceptions of prostitutes. Swinburne's woman, on the other hand, seems lulled and fortified by the indifference of her reflection to all but itself: 'Nought else exalts or grieves / The rose at heart, that heaves / With love of her own leaves and lips that pair.' As in the women's poetry, the speaker sees another self in the mirror, but this self has a plenitude and self-sufficiency she finds admirable. She encounters herself anew in a way that parallels Narcissus' discovery of himself in Ovid's *Metamorphoses* (3. 416–79) or Eve's rapture at her reflection in Milton's *Paradise Lost* (IV. 460–7). Yet, rather bizarrely one might think, narcissistic self-enjoyment seems attributed primarily to the woman's reflection rather than to the female speaker herself, although the woman then seems to enjoy and take strength from her reflection's pleasure – that is, she mirrors her reflection rather than her reflection mirroring her. Moreover, the lines 'The rose at heart, that heaves / With love of her own leaves and lips that pair' may also suggest that the mirror reflection delights in seeing herself reflected in the woman. Certainly the two seem bonded through a process of reinforcement and 'the lips that pair' may even hint at a reciprocal narcissistic kiss. This ambiguity about who mirrors whom is perhaps the reason why the woman asks 'Art thou the ghost, my sister, / White sister there, / Am I the ghost, who knows?' In the Romantic discourse of the mirror that Swinburne derived from Shelley, the reflection offers up an idealized, perfected or aesthetically enhanced view of reality; in the case of Swinburne's female speaker, it shows her as she would like to be. The mirror of art offers back reflection, shorn or devoid of troubled consciousness. The mirror image, unlike the woman, has no memory of past love affairs: 'She knows not loves that kissed her / She knows not where.'

It is the reflection's indifference to all but herself, her non-knowledge of past or future, which the woman finds attractive and restorative. The last line of the second stanza seems to show her absorbing that indifference: 'My hand, a fallen rose, / Lies snow-white on white snows, and takes no care.' Again Swinburne deftly uses floral imagery in an oblique and unsettling manner. To refer to a hand as 'a fallen rose' might simply be a picturesque way of referring to the woman's languid pose, to the hand perhaps resting on the white folds of her dress or on the white surround of the mantelpiece; but the flower image juxtaposed with 'snow-white' and 'fallen' is again troubling and, one wonders, is the 'hand' here a synecdoche for the woman herself? If the 'snow' that threatened the woman has entered the garden, her reverie in the mirror leaves her unconcerned. Again Swinburne's poem refuses a standard narrative about the 'fallen' woman in which she averts a fearful future by repenting her past. While popular practices of Victorian moral self-examination encouraged fallen women and others to meditate sombrely on their faulty personal histories, the final stanza of section two shows the woman's empowering identification with her reflection in which she discounts past and future in an act of self-reinforcement: 'But one thing knows the flower; the flower is fair.' The poem then at this point literalizes the act of reflection as an act of looking and appreciation rather than a process of moral recognition and regret. This section of the poem deliberately cuts against the emotional grain of Whistler's painting, insisting on seeing in the reflection a positive rather than a negative image, although its message of a love of the image for its own sake can also be seen as a sophisticated restatement of aesthetic formalism. The poem's title 'Before the Mirror' suggests that the poet, and even the reader, drawn into sympathy with the gazing woman and mesmerized by this scene of self-affirmation, may be seeing themselves through the restorative narcissism of the mirror. Swinburne must have known his poems would cause a scandal, and, in view of the fact that he was writing the poem to show his support for and solidarity with Whistler, an artist who had recently been critically attacked, 'Before the Mirror' could be read as consolatory and self-affirmatory as the poet defends himself from past or future attacks by gazing at the ideal poetic or artistic self.

If the second section of the poem insists on a certain kind of literalism, a love of the image for its own sake, the final section of the poem does something different. This concluding section seems more in line with the wistfulness of Whistler's imagery, although, while Whistler looks to the future, Swinburne looks more to the past. The woman in the poem also cuts a figure reminiscent of that famous embowered woman, Tennyson's Lady of Shalott, who, immured in her tower, can view the outside world only through its reflections in her mirror, reflections that she then translates into woven images. This process of viewing and re-creating the mirror images in woven form can be seen as the work of the writer or artist. The Lady's move away from the world of art to viewing and experiencing the real world results in her death. Swinburne's woman, who I think is also a figure for the artist or poet, does not suffer this fate; unlike Tennyson's Lady, she is experienced in love, and, in *her* mirror, it is the past rather than the present that she sees. Whereas in the previous section the woman claimed not to see her past, this section shows her staring into the glass, which acts as a sort of reservoir of past images. However, she is not shown as regretting or abjuring her past, but rather as reviewing philosophically its pleasures and pains, always aware of their transience. This material too seems to become the stuff of art. 'Deep in the gleaming glass / She sees all past things pass, / And all sweet life that was lie down and lie.' What does it mean for 'all sweet life that was' to 'lie down and lie' if not to become the fiction, the transformed work achieved by the mirror of art and the aesthetic observer? Whereas Tennyson's Lady forsakes the safe, enclosed and mediated world of art and is killed by the touch of reality or sexuality, Swinburne's woman turns her amorous experience into aesthetic reverie. All can be redeemed and reviewed in the dispassionate light of the mirror of art which allows ways of objectifying and aestheticizing one's past. Swinburne tells us his female gazer 'sees by formless gleams', recalling Wordsworth's famous use of this motif as a sign for the visionary imagination in the fled 'visionary gleam' of the *Intimations Ode* and the 'gleam that never was on sea or land' of the 'Elegiac Stanzas on Peele Castle'. Making art of one's life necessarily draws on echoes and images from existing art works, other poems, 'dreams that sing and sigh'. The river that runs past the Isle of Shalott becomes the 'cold streams' in the mirror, streams of consciousness that allow access to these dreamlike poems or songs of the past – for the past is heard as well as seen in this strangely synaesthetic mirror. This subsumption of personal experience by artistic form, convention and the literary tradition helps constitute the aesthetic self described earlier as 'impersonal'.

Although 'Before the Mirror' is constructed around a scene of defiant self-sufficency, it has nonetheless a noticeable melancholy, some of which permeates into the poem from its own literary 'past' dreams: 'The Lady of Shalott' and Shelley's 'To a Sky-Lark', which itself provided the germ of Tennyson's poem in its image of the embowered maiden, employed as an analogue for the out-of-reach sky-lark. Shelley's poem describes the happiness experienced by the bird, which seems inaccessible to humans, who, stricken with regrets, can never experience whole-hearted joy untainted by sorrow. Echoing the sentiment that 'Our sincerest gladness with some pain is fraught', Shelley's lyric manages to blend joy with wistfulness, whereas Swinburne's poem, which scatters and redistributes the language of Shelley's lyric, and fleetingly evokes its metre, is much more sombre. Both poems open with lines of three iambic feet, but Swinburne curtails the more upbeat movement of Shelley's lyric by following with a foreshortened line of two feet, which gives an oddly melancholic, slightly arrested feeling. Rather than straining to see the inaccessible sky-lark and trying to emulate its unblemished joy, Swinburne's woman concludes by focusing on her own past comprised of joys and sorrows, seeing that her own sad experiences echo or are part of all human grief, 'all men's tears beneath the sky'. While the poem ends on this sad note, it typically carries a note of Swinburneian resignation, which does not look for easy answers but acknowledges pain and disappointment as part of the human condition, yet at the same time refuses to be cowed by them, instead turning them into the fabric of art and poetry. Introspection, the dwelling on one's past, so often associated with the stock figure of the lovelorn or abandoned woman, is here reclaimed as an aesthetic act, and the figure of the isolated yet self-sufficient woman becomes an image of the detached and speculative artist.

If this poem, apparently only a decorative exercise, is actually a poem in which the 'fallen' and socially suspect woman doubles with the artist, then Swinburne revives this figure most powerfully in what could be seen to be his manifesto poem in *Poems and Ballads*: 'Sapphics'.[16] 'Sapphics' (Haynes, 163–5), also written probably in 1865, is one of several poems in this collection that honour Sappho, the woman Swinburne believed to be the supreme poet. Sappho, the classical Greek poet who lived on Lesbos, the epicentre of lyric poetry, around the seventh century BC (600 BC), has held a fascination for many of the poets who came after her. Plato called her 'the tenth muse', and she was known as 'the poetess', just as Homer was known as 'the poet'. She is said to be one of the first poets to write about the emotional complexities of personal relationships, and the first to comment on her place in futurity, her own poetic fame to come. We know little about the historical person of Sappho, although her poetry indicates that her romantic and sexual feelings were directed towards women. A later legendary tradition gives us the unsupported but popular story that she killed herself for the love of a young boatman, Phaon, by throwing herself from the Leucadian Cliff on Lesbos. This image of Sappho as a melancholy and disappointed woman-singer who kills herself for love was an enduring one that was much celebrated in eighteenth- and nineteenth-century poetry. It famously colours Tennyson's portrayals of melancholy or abandoned women in 'The Lady of Shalott', 'Mariana' and 'Mariana in the South'. Sappho's poems are prized for their lyrical grace and sensitivity, but they exist tantalizingly only in a fragmentary condition with very few pieces in anything like a complete state. Certain of Sappho's fragments were still being unearthed during the nineteenth century. It was said of Tennyson, a passionate admirer of Sappho, that the one thing he hoped for was the discovery of more of her poems.

From the seventeenth century onwards most of those people who imitated or admired Sappho either believed her to be or deliberately represented her as heterosexual. Swinburne, who was, of course, familiar with the classical sources, would have no truck with this sanitized version. His Sappho is quite explicitly a lesbian – one of the first open celebrations of lesbianism in English poetry since John Donne's fine poem 'Sappho to Philaenis'. Swinburne, following in the wake of the French poet Charles Baudelaire, who had written a number of poems exoticizing lesbianism, was not to be outdone. 'Anactoria', one of the most vilified poems in *Poems and Ballads,* is a declamation of sadomasochistic passion by Sappho to her lover Anactoria. It is also a profoundly philosophical poem about the relation between pain and pleasure, love and hate, which considers the nature of poetic fame, and the energies of nature and of the imagination. Here and in his other poems about her, Sappho is evidently very much Swinburne's own creation. Yet still it is with her voice, the voice of history's most famous woman poet, that he chooses to speak, and into her monologue he skilfully interpolates various of her poetic fragments. By impersonating Sappho, he takes on her mantle and lays claim to her poetic power and her immortality. At the same time he is anxious to redefine what Sappho and her legacy mean to him. The stock sentimentalized versions of Sappho are replaced by him with something much more redoubtable. Swinburne's Sappho is a formidable, an awe-inspiring presence. This is especially the case in 'Sapphics', which takes its name from the metrical four-line stanzas in which Sappho wrote her poems and which Swinburne also uses here. This is a difficult form to reproduce well in English. Classical metre is quantitative, measuring the duration of long and short Greek and Latin syllables, whereas English metre is predominantly accentual-syllabic, imposing patterns of stressed and unstressed syllables. Transposed into English the sapphic stanza consists of three eleven-syllable lines – hendecasyllables – followed by a five-syllable line. The stresses of the hendecasyllables imitate the quantities of the classical original and, in a 'pure' sapphic, the short line consists of a dactyl and a spondee. Swinburne's employment of the sapphic stanza in 'Sapphics' is generally thought to be the best example in English literature, for he is especially skilled, as Yopie Prins explains, in creating 'a stress analogue pattern that allows the long syllables in Greek to coincide, more or less, with stressed syllables in English'.[17]

It is easy to overlook the fact that there is a framing narrative to this poem. The poem opens with a vision or waking dream impressed upon the poet-speaker; an important detail, as I believe this scene of revelation is claimed by Swinburne as crucial to his poetry; or rather, as he artfully suggests, it claims him, in that he is compelled to witness and write about it. Notice how the speaker is the object of the personified attentions of first 'sleep', who obdurately withholds slumber, and then the 'vision', who touches him on his eyes and lips so that he can both see and then tell what he sees. This theme of compulsion will be central to the poem.

We are then introduced to the dramatic spectacle of Aphrodite, goddess of love, fleeing Mitylene in Lesbos, birthplace of Sappho, drawn in her chariot by her doves and followed by her winged attendants, the Loves. But curiously the doves are pictured looking back at what they flee, attracted by what repels them. The great noise made by the hasty departure of Aphrodite and her retinue is, however, counterpointed by another sound: the sound of women singing. At this point the poem takes us back to an earlier scene where we witness what has so alarmed Aphrodite. Sappho of Lesbos is portrayed in the midst of her female companions, singing her lyrical verse. Such is the power of her song that she outsings those guardians of song, Apollo's nine Muses, in an act of supremacy that literally enshrines her as the tenth, if not the only Muse, truly worth listening to. As the laurel crowns of the Muses fade, Sappho's forehead is illumined with a crown of everlasting fire to prove her immortality. Aphrodite's Loves have been moved to tears by her song and, in spite of herself, Aphrodite too is moved and urges Sappho to transfer her allegiance to her. But Sappho, immersed in her song, pays no attention to Aphrodite's sorrow. She has eyes only for her attendant women and their accompanying music, and her own song is so strongly realized it achieves a transcendent birdlike materiality:

> Newly fledged, her visible song, a marvel,
> Made of perfect sound and exceeding passion,
> Sweetly shapen, terrible, full of thunders,
>   Clothed with the wind's wings.

> (Haynes, 164)

Taking pleasure in her own song, she scatters roses, which are properly Aphrodite's signature blossom. At this point, the non-Lesbian audience composed of Muses, goddess and other divinities deserts Sappho; unable to bear her heart-searching song any longer, they flee her presence and Lesbos is left to its female singers. Then, suddenly moved forward in time, we are told that at certain twilight moments the neglected ghosts of these rejected female singers can still be heard inexorably revoicing their unconquerable and poignant melodies.

Why, we might wonder, is Aphrodite at odds with Sappho? In 'Sapphics' Swinburne is actually revising a poem of Sappho's known as the Ode to Aphrodite (Fragment 1) in which Sappho, distressed because the woman she loves is

43

ignoring her, prays that Aphrodite will help her. Aphrodite then enters the poem and humorously reminds Sappho that she has always helped her in the past and that the woman who is currently ignoring her will soon start pursuing her. In Sappho's original poem, then, Aphrodite is a friend and ally. But in his poem Swinburne makes Aphrodite exclusively into the goddess of heterosexual love, who is dismayed by Sappho's difference as a lover of women. Yet at the same time that difference is powerfully expressed in the love-poetry Sappho sings, which is so powerfully transcendent it touches the sympathetic emotions even of those who find its subject matter disturbing and repellent. That song is unconventional in that it is not sanctioned by any of the regular inspiring deities, the nine Muses, yet, at the same time, it does not need or seek their licensing authority, being equal to and far superior to them, and forcing them to admit its power. Aphrodite, entranced by the beauty of Sappho's song, urges her to turn her energies to celebrating heterosexual love, but Sappho, uninterested in what Aphrodite stands for, can acknowledge only the presence of her own women companions.

So what is Swinburne doing with this poem? Arguably it functions as a central statement of his vocation as a poet. Sappho is being used by Swinburne as a new version of the Romantic image of the artist as special, distinctive and thus different from most other people. The Romantic image usually suggests that, by virtue of his aesthetic abilities, heightened sensibility and unorthodox perspective on life, the artist is often a figure who is alienated from mainstream society. By using the figure of Sappho, Swinburne augments the sense of the artist's distinctiveness and deviance by stressing her gender and sexuality. The supreme singer is a woman who will have nothing to do with Victorian ideals of marriage, motherhood and domesticity. Sappho is also shown to be scattering roses, 'awful roses of holy blossom', traditionally associated with Aphrodite, and implying that her experience of love outranks that of the goddess. This is a triumphant gainsaying of conventionality, but at the same time it is touched with suffering as well. Sappho's song carries her famous mixed or 'bitter-sweet' emotional charge and thus contains suffering within it. Her 'ashen temples' are described as 'paler than grass in summer', an elegant translation of a moment in one of Sappho's most famous poems (Fragment 31) in which she says that the sight of the woman she loves laughing with a man makes her tremble and grow 'paler (or greener) than the grass'. The description of Sappho's pale forehead encircled by a crown of fire evokes iconographic images of the suffering Christ crowned with thorns, daringly suggesting her iconic status as a numinous figure who is despised and rejected. Swinburne's Sappho has a sort of tragic glamour as her gift is at once acknowledged and reviled and she and her women are effectively put beyond the pale. Thus the poem gives a picture of the brilliant socially alienated artist and predicts Swinburne's own sense of how the poet who speaks outside socially sanctioned themes, who tackles taboo subjects, will be treated. Such a literary artist may well be abhorred by society, but he or she cannot be ignored, as his or her considerable poetic gifts demand attention and acknowledgement. The poem also suggests how a new poetry, which springs from sources and subjects different from those of the mainstream, has the power to make more conventional subjects look dull and uninspired, just as Sappho's song fades the laurel crowns of the other Muses. The end of the poem speaks of the enduring legacy of such songs. Although anathematized by society, ghostly echoes that swell to imposing choruses can still be heard by those willing to listen.

So Swinburne in this poem is writing about how he sees the poet's role and the function of poetry. Identifying with Sappho, he also makes himself one with the ghosts of the outcast women whose singing revives her legacy. The audacious identification with Sappho is important in that she is a great poet and a sexual outsider, as was Swinburne himself. In 'Sapphics' and in other of his poems about Sappho, Swinburne compels his readers to look at something most of them would rather not acknowledge: the figure of the lesbian. While Swinburne's portrayals of lesbianism may not immediately appear very meaningful to a modern audience, seeming more the subject of imaginative fantasy, it should be noted that they had the virtue of making the lesbian visible, something that made Swinburne a hero to various Modernist lesbian writers such as H.D. and Renée Vivien. Following the example of Baudelaire in France, the poem also, in a modest way, helps to establish the modern sense of the word 'lesbian', shifting the word from its then dominant topographical connotation, into a more overt sexuality that would be recognized by Swinburne's classically educated contemporaries; indeed the *OED* cites Swinburne for the first use of the sexual term 'lesbianism' in 1869, four years after the publication of *Poems and Ballads*.

Baudelaire's lesbian poems might also be considered among the powerful songs sung by the 'outcast women', for 'Sapphics' owes something to 'Lesbos' and the two poems known as 'Femmes damnées' (the second also known as 'Delphine et Hippolyte'). 'Delphine et Hippolyte' and 'Lesbos' were among the six poems banned from subsequent publication after their initial appearance in *Les Fleurs du mal* (1857), and were not reprinted until 1866, when they appeared with some other poems in a limited press edition known as *Les Épaves*. Swinburne, who reviewed the second edition (1861) of *Les Fleurs du mal* in 1862, had apparently not read the banned works until William Michael Rossetti gave him a copy of the rare first edition in 1864, and it seems likely that 'Sapphics' was written the following year. The figure then of the recently contemned Baudelaire, arraigned for his treatment of lesbianism, thus also subliminally informs Swinburne's figure of the forsaken Sappho and her outcast women. Identifying with Baudelaire through the figure of Sappho and aware of the criticism that had been heaped on the hapless Meredith and others, Swinburne sees his own *Poems and Ballads* following the example of *Les Fleurs du mal* and anticipates his own public condemnation.

Baudelaire's first (unbanned) 'Femmes damnées' poem has the male speaker expressing sympathy for his 'poor sisters', women who suffer the pangs of unsatisfied same-sex desire. The second 'Femme damnées' ('Delphine et Hippolyte') describes the passion that exists between the two eponymous protagonists, which is seen as doomed and illicit and ends with a long lurid passage in which the women are consigned to hell, where as shades they will suffer the eternal torments of their unsatisfied desire. In 'Lesbos' the poet-speaker addresses the island itself, describing it as a place of beauty whose sexual customs fall outside the law. In sympathy with the ethos of the isle, he sees himself ordained to promote it, while he waits for the sea to return the body of Sappho, who flouted the rites of her cult when she slept with a man. Ever since Sappho's death Lesbos has been stricken and in mourning, 'drunk with the cries of torment which her deserted shores lift to the skies'. Swinburne's poem recalls and combines some of these scenarios in its sapphically sympathetic poet-narrator, and in its portrayal of the spectral outcast women who return to haunt Lesbos with their songs. But the expression of his sympathy for Sappho and her women is very different from Baudelaire's: he omits the note of condemnation that sounds in 'Delphine et Hippolyte', and, while the narrator of the first 'Femmes damnées' views his subjects in a rather patronizing and distanced way and the speaker of 'Lesbos' sets himself up as a self-acknowledged authority, the allegiance of Swinburne's speaker is implicit in his reverential eye-witness account of the scene of Sappho's supremacy. Of the three poems, 'Lesbos' probably has the greatest influence on 'Sapphics', for in that poem Baudelaire introduces the theme of a tension between Venus–Aphrodite and Sappho. The island of Lesbos is told that 'the galaxies of stars admire you no less than Paphos [the centre of Aphrodite's cult on Cyprus], and gave Venus good cause for envying Sappho', and Sappho herself is twice described as 'more beautiful than Venus'. Swinburne takes up this suggestion of rivalry and develops it into the more dramatic rift between Sappho and Aphrodite that we see enacted in 'Sapphics'. While his poem indirectly honours Baudelaire, it also perhaps signals his own rivalry with him. 'Sapphics' outdoes 'Lesbos' in that it is more 'authentically' sapphic, ignoring the 'impure' legend of the Lesbian poet's fatal passion for a man and expertly emulating Sappho's own metre.

While he celebrates her as a sexual outsider, Swinburne always tends to portray Sappho as partly tragic, not merely because she is rejected by society but because she seems frequently frustrated in her loves, who appear faithless and fleeting. In this too he takes a hint from Baudelaire, who in 'Lesbos' describes Sappho as deathly pale and marked by the signs of grief, implying her melancholy status as 'lover and poet'. For Swinburne, there is the sense that she represents the type of the artist who is successful in her art (an art stimulated by her sexual desire) but is less successful in her relationships. In this she has an affinity with Swinburne himself. An early lost love, now widely believed to be his cousin Mary Gordon, and masochistic tendencies that could not be relieved by a regular Victorian marriage put an end to hope of a lasting romantic or sexual relationship. Lesbianism and other forms of non-reproductive sexuality in Swinburne are often referred to as 'fruitless' and 'barren', as he draws a distinction between the heterosexual world of regular fruitful reproductivity, which is deemed inferior in terms of its artistic productions, and a creative sphere, stimulated by unconventional sexual desires, which brings forth immortal artworks but cannot beget children or provide more immediate forms of earthly satisfaction. Swinburne would later regretfully write to Gosse of the early disappointment in love that left his 'young manhood "a barren stock" ' (*Letters*, iii. 51). The feeling of a gift won at great cost or personal sacrifice perhaps also informs the tragic atmosphere that concludes the poem.

More significantly, perhaps, the poem also describes the way in which Swinburne wanted his poems to work on his readers. Swinburne was consciously following the principle of art for art's sake that he had inherited from Théophile Gautier and Baudelaire, which makes the aesthetic aspect of the work of art of the highest, if not the only importance, and allows the artist legitimately to tackle any topic he chooses, regardless of how shocking or reprehensible it may be, so long as he produces something artistically beautiful. The French Aestheticist belief that a dubious subject matter could be partnered by beautiful style was at this time unfamiliar in England. Robert Buchanan, one of Swinburne's most virulent critics, voiced the popular belief when he declared in an essay on literary morality 'a true lover of books knows well that what is really shocking will not attract him, because it is sure to be shockingly – i.e. inartistically uttered'.[18] Swinburne's earliest critics were thus deeply disturbed by the fact that Swinburne's verse did not obey this critical commonplace and that they could not fault him on his use of form or language, which was beautifully handled. In 'Sapphics', Sappho's song is portrayed as having the aesthetic capability to engage readerly sympathy in that its extreme power and beauty sway even her strongest opponents, who are moved to tears. The poem dramatizes the way in which Swinburne hoped his poetry would work on his readers. As I said in introducing the poem, it is about compulsion. Swinburne's poet-speaker is compelled by the vision and Sappho's hearers are compelled by her song, just as Swinburne hoped that his own readers would be compelled by his poetry, and this poem in particular, with its consummate use of metre, its witty dialogue with classical and contemporary literature, and its skilful and sophisticated scene setting.

'PASIPHAE'

A further example of this process of compulsion and sympathetic conversion can be seen in my third poem, the dramatic fragment 'Pasiphae', unpublished during Swinburne's lifetime and reprinted for the first time for a general audience in the Appendix to this book. With the British Library manuscript watermarked 1867, 'Pasiphae' looks as if it was written as a belated partner poem for 'Phædra' in *Poems and Ballads*.[19] Both poems deal with episodes from the Greek myths of King Minos and Theseus, although in terms of the narrative 'Pasiphae' is chronologically earlier. Pasiphae is the wife of Minos, by whom she has daughters Phædra and Ariadne. Ariadne helps the Greek hero Theseus to slay the famous Minotaur, but, after Theseus cruelly abandons her on the island of Naxos, it is Phædra who eventually marries him. The Minotaur, a ferocious creature half-man half-beast, is bizarrely the half-brother of both girls, being the product of Pasiphae's infatuation for a white bull. She had been afflicted with this unnatural lust by the god Poseidon, who was angry with Minos for withholding the bull as a sacrifice to him. The Minotaur was confined in the famous labyrinth designed by the inventor Daedalus, where it was offered a yearly sacrificial tribute of fifty young men and fifty maidens. Although the myth is treated by a number of classical writers, Swinburne's 'Pasiphae' is not indebted to any particular narrative source; concentrating on the early stages of the queen's infatuation, it tells how she yearns to consummate her passion and how Daedalus helps her achieve her desire.[20] Although 'legitimated' by classical myth, the subject matter went beyond even the licence of *Poems and Ballads*, ensuring that the poem was not published during Swinburne's lifetime. It has subsequently been printed in two rare limited press editions available to only a handful of readers with the result that it is virtually unknown.

Pasiphae, however, is not entirely absent from *Poems and Ballads*; one among the procession of legendary women in 'The Masque of Queen Bersabe' who testify to the power of female sexual allure and passion, she makes a short cryptic speech about the overwhelming nature of her fatal desire:

> I am the queen Pasiphae.
> Not all the pure clean-coloured sea
>   Could cleanse or cool my yearning veins;
>
> .   .   .   .
>
> From shame's pressed core I wrung the sweet
> Fruit's savour that was death to eat,
>   Whereof no seed but death remains.
>
> (Haynes, 184)

In 'Phædra', Pasiphae's daughter, stricken by Aphrodite with an incestuous infatuation for her stepson Hippolytus, rues her troubled family history and alludes obliquely to her mother's shameful liaison. Ate, goddess of evil, she says,

> hath sown pain and plague in all our house,
> Love loathed of love, and mates unmatchable,
> Wild wedlock, and the lusts that bleat or low,
> And marriage-fodder snuffed about of kine.
>
> (Haynes, 28)

Maddened by her desire, she concludes the poem by wishing that she had been among the maidens sacrificed to the Minotaur:

> I would I had been the first that took her death
> Out from between wet hoofs and reddened teeth,
> Splashed horns, fierce fetlocks of the brother bull!
>
> (Haynes, 28)

When John Morley wrote his condemnatory review of *Poems and Ballads*, he picked up on these traces of Pasiphae's story, citing her as the ultimate name in a list that signifies unspeakable female depravity: 'It is not everybody who would care to let the world know that he found the most delicious food for poetic reflection in the practices of the great island of the Ægean, in the habits of Messalina, of Faustina, of Pasiphaë' (*SCH* 23). Bayard Taylor, writing to fellow American critic E. C. Stedman on 24 April 1867 about Swinburne's 'weak moral sense', commented: 'He told me some things, unspeakably shocking, which he had omitted from his last volume' (*SCH* 8). This omitted matter could well be 'Pasiphae', something that Taylor finds too repugnant even to name. Even today the ostensible topic of 'Pasiphae' – bestiality – is not the easiest to discuss. And yet, the poem works by typical Swinburneian movements of compulsion and sympathetic conversion, so that it does, following the Baudelairean principle, indeed disarm the reader and offer itself as food for poetic reflection.

The form Swinburne uses is clearly influenced by Greek dramatic models, and the poem simulates a translation of a classical text. Fragments survive of a play featuring Pasiphae by Euripides called *The Cretans*, but Swinburne's dramatic fragment, too sexually transgressive in its language to pass as an authentic Greek tragedy, may possibly have been influenced by the genre known as the 'satyr-play', a semi-comic drama in which the chorus led by Silenus was always composed of satyrs wearing horses' tails and ears. At the Athenian drama festivals each trilogy of tragedies would have been followed by a satyr-play by the same author, the play consisting of a bawdy burlesque of some mythological episode derived from the preceding trilogy. Only one example of the genre still survives: Euripides' *The Cyclops*. In spite of his much-vaunted dislike of Euripides, Swinburne showed himself familiar with this play to the extent that, when Shelley's editor William Michael Rossetti was annotating the poet's translation of the play, Swinburne supplied him with translations of bawdy lines that had been omitted (2 December 1869; *Letters*, ii. 61–2). While Swinburne's 'Pasiphae' is not burlesque or comic in nature, its pronounced sexual character suggests it may have been inspired by this tradition. And yet, as with

51

other of his poems that treat sexually illicit topics, there is no overt use of erotically explicit or obscene language. At one point in their dialogue, Daedalus, anxious to avert the possible enmity of the gods, tells Pasiphae: 'Keep thy tongue wary & choose innocuous words' (l. 63). It could be a watchword for the poem, which negotiates its subject matter with a self-delighting deftness. Pasiphae's dilemma, the solution proposed by Daedalus and his explanation of it to her are relayed gradually and in language that gracefully and artfully flirts with the reader's knowledge of the sexual scenario, simultaneously veiling and unveiling it through euphemism, circumlocution, metaphor and *double entendre* while rousing sexual awareness through neatly deployed paronomastic phrases such as 'the cunning carved beast' (l. 5) (evoking the Latin *cunna* 'vulva') or 'amorous will / Pricks to the bone' (ll. 20–1). This subtle teasing is itself provocative, piquing sexual curiosity and appealing to voyeurism. Taking care not to alienate its readers, the poem seductively draws them into the drama, where they are made a hidden third party to Daedalus' tactful explanations to Pasiphae. What preoccupies Swinburne is not Pasiphae's specific lust for the bull – there is comparatively little interest shown in the animal himself – but her yearning to slake her powerful desire for penetration, the bull being simply the optimal means to that end.

Centred by a fierce female desire for sexual satisfaction, the poem seems obsessed with interiors and inner space: the parching thirst and genital ache of Pasiphae's desiring body expressed as a 'wider-waxing wound' (l. 22), her troubled, obsessed consciousness, the ingenious mind of Daedalus as revealed in his solution, and the very inside of the decoy cow he devises for Pasiphae so that she can surreptitiously take her pleasure. These interiors seem to merge oddly, and with the oddest effect on the reader, as Daedalus enlightens Pasiphae as to the use of the decoy. As he explains how she can get inside the decoy and position herself for intercourse, there is the most curious sense that the reader too is being inducted, entering not merely into the requisite know-how, but into an inner space that communicates with the mind, body and physical desire of the queen herself. By a kind of empathetic process, the revelation made by Daedalus to the excitedly responsive

Pasiphae makes the reader imaginatively assimilate her condition. Sympathy, which can cross and blur boundaries and helps one individual get inside the situation of another, here makes for a disturbingly powerful literalization, as Pasiphae has the reader share in her preoccupation. This manœuvre is typically part of Swinburne's perverse poetics of sympathy, as through the blandishments of style, rhetoric and narrative dexterity he seduces the compliant reader into accepting a situation and a consciousness that he or she would normally find antipathetic.

Daedalus, too, is as much mediator for the unwitting reader as he is Pasiphae's guide and mentor, for it is he who opens the poem with a vividly sympathetic description of her sexual torment. This account contrasts with the lament of Pasiphae's nurse at the end of the dramatic fragment, where she bewails her mistress's condition. Both Daedalus and the nurse are sympathetic, but the nurse is an anxious and appalled observer while Daedalus' vivid narration of Pasiphae's symptoms and their cure give the impression that he has imaginatively entered her psyche and experienced her physical cravings. The physical immediacy of the sensations he imagines for her – the 'strong drink of salt-tasted love' (l. 10), 'Sweet stings & pleasurable warm violences / And shoots of fluid flame through the aching blood' (ll. 16–17), 'the sharp goad of an amorous will ... biting her flesh with teeth' (ll. 20–1) – suggests that he has fantasized himself as occupying her bodily consciousness. In contrast with the measured, doom-laden, almost elegiac tones used by the nurse, the visceral quality of Daedalus' language shows him to be a superb inventor who inhabits Pasiphae's problem while using his imaginative energies to devise a solution that will give her satisfaction. Moreover, borders get blurred in the ensuing conversation. As Daedalus is explaining to Pasiphae precisely how she should use the decoy, she quickly perceives his meaning, and the ensuing stichomythia is a fast-paced exchange of elegant sexual innuendo in which both parties effortlessly continue each other's lines and metaphors, revealing themselves to be of one mind. In this and in his preliminary devising, Daedalus performs an unexpectedly graphic version of erotic sympathy that looks like a parody of the conventional Victorian sympathetic ideal. He also provides an interesting example of a man projecting himself into an imagined female consciousness and, as such, represents in cameo what Swinburne as poet has done in 'Pasiphae' and does elsewhere in his poems about women. It is probable that Swinburne would have shared the unpublished 'Pasiphae' only with a small group of male associates. Thus, if Daedalus mediates Pasiphae's story, providing an example of what it is to be a sympathetic reader, he pitches this example at a readership that is most likely male. Such readers, emulating Daedalus, find themselves not merely sympathetic but feminized, partners to Pasiphae's desires and fantasies.

The poem also performs another mischievous literalization upon the word 'fit', which occurs in various different forms throughout the poem. The Victorian concern with what is fit matter for literature, for publication, is travestied by the couple's concern with the fitness, the design or potential effectiveness, of the decoy and its fit, the easy accommodation of Pasiphae. What is fitting has nothing to do with moral questions and everything to do with physical requirements and satisfaction. More generally, as we saw earlier, fitness for Swinburne is also something to do with choosing the right form to suit the subject. With regard to Baudelaire's provocative subject matter, he comments: 'Only supreme excellence of words will suffice to grapple with and fitly render the effects of such material . . . such things are unfit for rapid or careless treatment' (SAC 30). Just as Pasiphae needs Daedalus' extreme skill as an inventor to create the form she needs to achieve her desire, so controversial topics need the hand of a consummate poetic craftsman who can make the words fit the subject in such a way as to disarm the resistant reader. Thus 'Pasiphae', a poem in which Swinburne 'fitly now sets fit word to word' (ll. 55), proves to be a particularly fine example of the way in which 'the author deemed fit for poetical treatment certain passional aspects of human life concerning which the best English tradition had hitherto been one of reticence' (SCH 208).

2

Swinburne's Poetry up to 1878

'Hesperia', one of the last poems composed for *Poems and Ballads* (1866), documents a turning-away from the deliberately histrionic excesses of 'Dolores'. In this reflective eventide poem, the speaker, tired of passion, has a vision of his first love, a woman of wistful beauty, ' "Hesperia", the tenderest type of woman or of dream, born in the westward "isles of the blest" ' ('Notes on Poems and Reviews', Haynes, 408; *SR* 23), and a foil for the voracious *femme fatale* who symbolizes the lusts he now wishes to escape. The visionary woman has, he thinks, 'Come back to redeem and release me from love that recalls and represses, / That cleaves to my flesh as a flame, till the serpent has eaten his fill' ('Hesperia', Haynes, 141). Even as he tries to elude the temptress he calls 'Dolores', he is still aware of her magnetic, cruelly consuming charms, and appeals to 'Hesperia' to flee with him into the future on the 'swift horses of fear or of love', a frantic race whose outcome is as yet uncertain: 'And our spirits too burn as we bound, thine holy but mine heavy-laden, / As we burn with the fire of our flight; ah love, shall we win at the last?' (Haynes, 144).

Two remarkable poems continue this allegorical treatment of the development of the poet: the 'Prelude' to *Songs before Sunrise* (1871) and 'Thalassius' from *Songs of the Springtides* (1880). The first of these tells how 'Youth', a figure full of aspirations, is sidetracked by the temptation to pursue pleasure and write verse about it. But Swinburne's narrator is indulgent about this – 'Play then and sing; we too have played' – knowing it to be only an agreeable interlude. The wild music of self-indulgence will eventually fall silent, 'For Pleasure slumberless and pale, / And Passion with rejected veil, / Pass'

(*PS* ii. 7). The soul, which the narrator calls 'man's God', cannot, however, be defeated by change or time, and, if heeded as a guide, will allow the individual to live out his potential in ways that help secure the freedom of all souls. 'Thalassius' fleshes out these transitions with a more evidently semi-autobiographical narrative. The eponymous hero is the child of a sea-nymph, Cymothoe, and Apollo, God of the sun and of poetry. Found as a baby on the seashore, his spiritual home, the child is raised by a poet foster-father (often identified as Landor, one of Swinburne's poetic idols) who teaches him about liberty, and love, hate, hope and fear. Embarking on his life's journey, the youth encounters the god Love for himself, but it is a painful meeting and saddens his spirit. When he is overtaken by a Dionysian throng of revellers, he loses his sadness by throwing himself into the pursuit of pleasure. For a time oblivious of his former life, he eventually tires of the revel and falls asleep on the shore, and in sleep recovers his early aspirations. Finally he is blessed by his father Apollo, who honours him for feeding 'men's hearts with visions, truer than truth' (*PS* iii. 10), and blesses him with the gift of the song of the elemental life force.

These three poems in different ways represent Swinburne's need to move on from the more sensual and erotic themes of *Poems and Ballads* to new subject matter. In the first instance that subject matter would be political, but this change of direction was, as 'Prelude' and 'Thalassius' hint, a return to former ideals. First among these was his dedication to the Italian political uprising known as the Risorgimento ('resurrection'), whose goal was a free united Italy. Those who identify whole-heartedly with another's cause generally do so because that cause has a powerful symbolic value for them. Sandra Gilbert famously suggested that the Risorgimento was significant for various Victorian women poets, and in particular Elizabeth Barrett Browning, because Italy's resurrection paralleled the woman poet's own resurrection and coming-into-strength.[1] Swinburne, wishing to transcend the eroticism and art-for-art's-sake attitudes perceived as characteristic of *Poems and Ballads*, also saw the Risorgimento as an opportunity for redefining himself and reviving earlier aspirations. The erotic sympathy of *Poems and Ballads* now gives way to the political and libertarian sympathies of a new collection, *Songs before Sunrise* (1871), in which the poet disregards the boundaries of his own national identity to share in the emancipatory struggles of other countries. Italy's struggle especially is viewed by Swinburne as a sublime scene of suffering and redemption in which he as poet is intimately involved, and it is this sense of sympathetic participation and involvement that he wishes to engender in his readers.

ITALY AND *SONGS BEFORE SUNRISE* (1871)

Italy, beloved by many British writers and travellers, was a country ripe for liberation in that it had never been a free and united nation under its own national ruler or government, but was instead a collection of states. Many of these had at one time been ruled by other nations such as France, Spain and, after the Treaty of Utrecht in 1713, Austria, while the central Papal States were governed from Rome by the Pope. Trade barriers separated the states, as did differences in currency, weights and measures and peasant dialects that could not be understood outside specific regions. Such divisions held back industrialization. Standards of living were extremely variable from one part of the country to another, and, with the exception of the small republic of San Marino, ordinary people had no vote or share in the government of the states, which was carried out by rulers and their chosen ministers. There was little popular education, with the result that illiteracy was widespread. Ironically, when the then-general Napoleon Bonaparte invaded Italy in 1796, thereafter introducing French administration and better conditions to the whole country, the Italians had their first taste of what it might be like to be a nation. After Napoleon had been defeated, when the results of French occupation had been erased and the former powers restored, many began to long for a united democratic Italy. Those longings were translated into political activism by the Italian republican Giuseppe (Joseph) Mazzini (1805–72). Rejecting the former revolutionary underground movement, the Carbonari, as outdated, lacking vision, and dominated by old and middle-aged leaders, Mazzini, who had been exiled to

France for his insurgency, founded in July 1831 the 'Young Italy' movement, which recruited supporters among men under 40 for 'one free independent republican nation'. Giuseppe Garibaldi (1807–82), the most famous of these recruits, would become a brilliant and daring commander, responsible for the key military campaigns to secure and defend Italy's liberation. In 1837 the exiled Mazzini came to England, where he continued his work for the Italian nationalist cause, becoming well known for his articles on literature and politics, and gaining many influential English supporters, a number of whom made parliamentary representations when the British Government was discovered to have interfered with his personal mail. Mazzini would remain on English soil for most of his life, apart from absences to organize revolutionary activity and, when Pope Pius IX was temporarily ousted in 1849, to head a short-lived Roman republic.[2]

Swinburne had long nursed an admiration for Mazzini and, while still an undergraduate, had penned an ode in his honour. At Oxford, where one of his teachers, Aurelio Saffi, was a friend and supporter of Mazzini's, Swinburne had also been strongly influenced by the republicanism of his close friend John Nichol and of other fellow members in the 'Old Mortality' debating society. Moreover, he venerated Felice Orsini for his attempt in January 1858 to assassinate the tyrannical Louis Napoleon (nephew of Bonaparte), who had become Emperor of France in 1852.[3] *Poems and Ballads* had included some explicitly political verse such as 'A Song in Time of Order. 1852' (which attacks Napoleon III's rise to imperial power) and 'A Song in Time of Revolution. 1860' (which celebrates Garibaldi's successful offensive in Central and Southern Italy), although these poems were overshadowed by the more sexually sensational material. In October 1866, after Venice had been freed from Austrian rule, Swinburne started writing 'a little song of gratulation . . . with due reserves and anticipations' intended to conclude with 'some not quite inadequate expression of reverence towards Mazzini' (9 October 1866; *Letters*, i. 195), which would turn into the many pages of 'A Song of Italy'. On meeting Mazzini in late March 1867 Swinburne read him the entire poem while sitting at his feet, and it was subsequently published with an admiring dedication. Mazzini's injunction to 'Give us a series of "Lyrics for the Crusade" ' (*Letters*, i. 236 n.) would be instrumental in encouraging Swinburne to produce the poems that make up *Songs before Sunrise*.

Edmund Gosse remarks: 'We are not accustomed in the history of literature to find a poet so passionately excited about problems of statecraft which do not affect his own life in any way, and with the results of which he will never be brought in contact' (*Life*, 191–2). But this is to ignore the considerable sympathy voiced from the 1840s onward by many liberal middle- and upper-class English men and women for the Italian Republican cause and for the charismatic Mazzini in particular.[4] The Ashhursts, a middle-class English family who befriended Mazzini in 1845 and thereafter supported his political activities, provide a good example, as does the poet Harriet Hamilton-King (1840–1920), author of poems about Orsini and Garibaldi, who was arguably just as passionate about Italian unification with as little 'real' cause or gain as was Swinburne. Certainly Swinburne, who had had a cult of Mazzini since he was 15 (*Letters*, i. 195), would have followed political developments in Italy in good company. As Samuel Chew writes, he 'passed his youth in the years of struggle, defeat, and renewed struggle; and the events of the *Risorgimento* sank deep into his memory, became part of himself'.[5] Swinburne's sympathetic incorporation of the Italian cause is reflected in his feelings about *Songs before Sunrise*, which he always thought the best of his writings, calling it 'my ripest and carefullest – and out of sight my most personal and individual – work' (4 March 1871; *Letters*, ii. 138), remarking later 'my other books are books, *Songs before Sunrise* is myself' (22 July 1875; *Letters*, iii. 35).

One of the seeming problems of *Songs before Sunrise* is that Swinburne emerged as a poet of the Italian cause late in the day, as the struggle was coming to a close. The goal had been the reunification of Italy and the attainment of liberty through republican government. In 1867, when Swinburne met Mazzini, unification had very nearly been achieved, if regrettably under the monarchy in the person of King Victor Emmanuel. However, while Rome still remained apart and under the control of the Pope, there was a hope that Mazzini might win it over to become a democratic republic, which might then spread throughout a unified Italy. This hope gave *Songs before Sunrise* a particular focus, but the volume would be outstripped by the passage of events. The bulk of the poems had been written before October 1868. Only six were published at the time of composition, and completion of the volume, followed by troubles with publishers, delayed publication until April 1871.[6] This had the effect of making topical poems and, indeed, the collection as a whole seem somewhat irrelevant to contemporary readers, especially as Italian unification had been achieved in September 1870, when Rome had been removed from the Pope's sovereignty and proclaimed the capital of Italy. Although the formation of an Italian republic would have to wait until after the Second World War, Italy's identity as a nation was now established. By the time that Swinburne's first serious critics came to evaluate his life's work in the early twentieth century, the events of this period of history already seemed obscure and beside the point in the light of later political developments. Arguably the belatedness of the collection and its seeming lack of relevance to the subsequent events of the nineteenth century may matter less to a modern reader, who can still appreciate the powerful symbolic function of the poetry, and indeed not all the poems concern Italy. There are addresses to France ('Quia Multum Amavit'), Greece ('Ode on the Insurrection in Candia'), and England ('An Appeal', 'Perinde Ac Cadaver'); considerations on the more general theme of European and global democracy, and a number of philosophical pieces that emphasize liberty as the precondition for meaning in human life and the sacred power and potential of the autonomous human spirit ('Hertha', 'Tenebræ', 'The Pilgrims', 'Hymn of Man, 'On the Downs'). A small group of poems address inspiring libertarian figures such as Mazzini ('Dedication', 'A New Year's Message', 'Epilogue'), Shelley ('Cor Cordium'), Victor Hugo ('Eurydice'), Walt Whitman, and the French republican and insurrectionary Armand Barbès. Nonetheless it is also true that many of the *Songs before Sunrise* and other of Swinburne's political verses cry out for some careful historical annotation, which would explain their specific contexts. Good preliminary overviews can be found in the sympathetic treatments by Georges Lafourcade and Samuel

Chew, which provide some useful contextual and background information, and can be supplemented by valuable insights from later critics such as Jerome McGann, Ross C. Murfin, Margot Louis and Alison Milbank.

Although often sidelined by readers, *Songs before Sunrise* nonetheless lends itself to a number of underexplored interpretative possibilities. Nationalist political poetry is still a neglected critical topic, although it is pertinent to remember that the distinguished historian of the Risorgimento, G. M. Trevelyan, was warm in his enthusiasm for Swinburne's republican poetry, calling 'The Halt before Rome' 'the finest political rhapsody in our language'.[7] More analysis is needed of the ways in which Swinburne strives to turn his considerable lyrical gifts to political ends and specifically to the task of rousing transnational sympathy in his readers. Alternatively one might seek to re-establish a broader sociocultural context for the poems, as in Stephanie Kuduk's recent essay, which reads *Songs before Sunrise* through the lenses of British 'republican aesthetics', seeing it as emerging from 'the vibrant culture of republicanism in the 1860s and 1870s, a culture that nourished republican poetry as well as democratic politics, and that viewed poetry as a central agent of political change'.[8] In such a reading the poetry is not belated or irrelevant but is very much a vital reflection of democratic and egalitarian concerns current in radical British thinking. This reading is strengthened by the fact that Mazzini had always seen the liberation of Italy as the first step towards world revolution and brotherhood, and it is clear that Swinburne too sees Italy's struggle as archetypal or exemplary, a glorious example of things to come. Poems such as 'The Eve of Revolution' and 'The Litany of Nations' plainly envisage a new world order. In 'The Eve of Revolution' the speaker adjures his native land 'Build up our one Republic state by state, / England with France, and France with Spain, / And Spain with sovereign Italy strike hands and reign' (*PS* ii. 20). With regard to the issue of influences, Terry Meyers has thoughtfully examined Swinburne's response to Shelley's republicanism in *Songs before Sunrise*, but one might also see the collection as very much influenced by Elizabeth Barrett Browning, Swinburne's chief poetic progenitor in the cause of Italian freedom. Swinburne had always been a great admirer of Barrett Browning, being warm in praise for her *Aurora Leigh* while still a student at Oxford (*Letters*, i. 10), and, in 'The Halt before Rome', he refers to her pro-nationalist poetry as 'the sweet great song that we heard / Poured upon Tuscany' and the poet herself as a 'Sea-eagle of English feather, / A song-bird beautifully souled' (*PS* ii. 46, 247). He does, however, take issue with her support for King Victor Emmanuel, whom he elsewhere referred to as 'the hog-faced Savoyard' and 'that satellite of a dead dog' (*Letters*, ii. 125), and he deplored her advocacy of Napoleon III. Alison Milbank has recently favourably compared Swinburne's Miltonic sonnet 'In San Lorenzo' with the poetic passage by Barrett Browning that inspired it, the Medici tomb section of *Casa Guidi Windows*, noting that it 'expresses in fourteen lines nearly as much as Browning in four times as many', but clearly there remains room for more detailed work on the relationship between the two poets.[9]

One area ripe for exploration is Swinburne's feminization of the key allegorical figures in his poems. Various of Swinburne's critics have suggested that this is simply a matter of transforming the formidable yet fascinating *femmes fatales* and female divinities of *Poems and Ballads* into the rather less appealing (because more austere) forms of Italia and Liberty.[10] But this is to simplify and trivialize the matter, for, as Sandra Gilbert noted, 'The trope of Italy or of one of "her" city states as a living, palpable, and often abandoned woman had become almost ubiquitous by the time Barrett Browning began to write her poems about the risorgimento.' Gilbert claimed, however, that Barrett Browning and other women writers revive the trope of Italy as woman 'to transform Italy ... from a problematic country in Europe to the problem condition of femaleness'.[11] Yet, as Alison Chapman has recently pointed out, in *Casa Guidi Windows* Barrett Browning specifically decried the personification of Italy as a vulnerable, feeble, suffering woman.[12] Notably Swinburne's female personifications avoid this stereotype. They are intended to rouse sympathy but not through pity alone. As various critics, Margot Louis chief among them, have shown, Swinburne, intimately acquainted with Scripture from his Anglo-Catholic upbringing, often recycled biblical language and Christian iconography for his own ends. He had already parodied the litany of the Blessed Virgin Mary in 'Dolores', and in *Songs before Sunrise* he uses Marian typology to more serious purpose. Both Italy and Liberty are seen as holy mother figures who engender or demand sympathy, and in Swinburne's scheme the figure of Christ is replaced by the sorrowful mother herself who undergoes suffering and resurrection. Italy (or the Republic or Liberty) is a *mater dolorosa*, a noble woman who suffers bravely and inspires action, or, alternately, having attained victory, a *mater triumphalis*. The opening of 'Super Flumina Babylonis' recalls Psalm 137, in which the exiled Jews in Babylon mourn the loss of Israel, this Old Testament reference forming a parallel to the plight of Italy crushed by her oppressors. Yet this mellifluous poem goes on to relate the rise of the 'Young Italy' movement under the influence of Mazzini, and, using a New Testament parallel, literalizes the Risorgimento in the imagery of the crucifixion and glorious resurrection of mother Italy.

Gilbert suggested the importance of Italy as a nurturant motherland to Barrett Browning, but it would also seem that this is true for Swinburne too, who saw it as the place where his imaginative energies were newly invested. The maternal nature of Italy, like the maternal nature of the sea, is often stressed in his poetry and, like the sea, may find a source in childhood associations. His devotion to Italy was almost certainly absorbed from his own mother, who taught him Italian while he was still a boy and monitored his early reading. It was she who took him to visit the poet Samuel Rogers (1763–1855), author of *Italy* (1822–8) in 1852, explaining to Rogers that she did so because her son 'thinks more of poets than of any other people in the world'. At this meeting, Rogers, who had recently turned down the laureateship on account of his great age, famously prophesied that the young Algernon would be a poet, an event that Swinburne later declared confirmed his calling (Gosse, *Life*, 23–4). Lady Jane thus seems to have been instrumental in promoting her son's love for Italy and assuring his vocation as a poet. Swinburne would have been nearly 15 at this meeting, which thus narrowly pre-dates his hero-worship of Mazzini, and it is possible Rogers's poetry may have helped shape his Italian sympathies, for Rogers had been described by Mazzini as 'the first Englishman who foretold that there would yet arise a third Italy'.[13]

If domestic associations provide the germ for Swinburne's images of Italy as mother, these are doubtless strengthened by Mazzini's beliefs in the importance of the inspiring feminine. Mazzini was also devoted to his mother, a highly intelligent woman who supported his political aims, and this had helped determine his high opinion of the female sex. He instructed his male readers to 'Love and respect Woman. Seek in her not merely a comfort, but a force, an inspiration, the redoubling of your intellectual and moral faculties. Cancel from your minds every idea of superiority over Women. You have none whatsoever.' Believing woman to be the primary source of education for all citizens, he also told them that 'the *Emancipation of Women*, then, must be regarded by you as necessarily linked with the emancipation of the Working-man'.[14] He had strong friendships with many British women and supported the English movements for female suffrage, and a sizeable number of his followers were active in the fight to enfranchise women. One of these was the widowed Emily Ashhurst Venturi, whom Mazzini hoped might inspire Swinburne to abandon his irregular lifestyle; this was not to be, although the poet spoke of her reverently as 'a chosen sister and as an exceptional woman'.[15] Another was Jessie White Mario, praised by Swinburne's *alter ego* Redgie Harewood in *A Year's Letters* for her 'splendid labour' in nursing the troops during Garibaldi's military campaign of 1860 (*AYL* 117). Woman as the champion of freedom evidently struck a chord with Swinburne, who idolized Emily Brontë and would later, on more than one occasion, eulogize her poem 'The Old Stoic' because of its demand for liberty (see *SAC* 205). The late 1860s, when Swinburne was writing *Songs before Sunrise*, was a period when the issue of women's emancipation began to receive serious attention. In 1867 John Stuart Mill, whose book *On Liberty* Swinburne greatly admired (*Letters*, i. 197), proposed unsuccessfully in parliamentary debates on the possible extension of the franchise that the word 'man' in the bill be replaced by the word 'person'; two years later in 1869 he published 'The Subjection of Women', written in 1861 with the help of his wife Harriet Taylor Mill. It thus seems likely that Swinburne's personifications of Italy and Liberty as suffering yet forcefully participating in the struggle for freedom are informed by the contemporary agitation for female emancipation supported by Mazzinian libertarian ideals.

A notable cluster of female types occurs in Swinburne's poem 'Siena', one of the finest poems in *Songs before Sunrise*, which details the narrator's reflections on the plight of Italy, when, during an English summer, he casts his mind back to time spent in Siena, 'the lovely city of my love' (*PS* ii. 160). In this poem we meet in turn the personified spirit of Siena herself, followed by St Catherine of Siena, protector of her people, glorified in frescoes by Sodoma (Giovanni Antonio Bazzi, 1477–1549) in the Church of San Domenico. These images recall another painting by Sodoma in the nearby Sienese Academy, of the tortured Christ, which prompts the narrator's pity, along with contempt for the way Church and State have traduced his teaching.[16] He turns away to the contrastingly lovely sight of the antique sculptured group of the Three Graces, but finds this image of Grecian serenity and sensuality out of place in a country torn apart by conflict. In the twilight he hears the plaint of a former native of Siena, Dante's La Pia, murdered by her husband, asking to be remembered (' "*Ricorditi di me*" '), a cry that is then taken up by the voice of the spirit of enfettered Italy, whose sufferings are compared to those of Christ:

> With other face, with speech the same,
> A mightier maiden's likeness came
> Late among mourning men that slept,
> A sacred ghost that went and wept,
> White as the passion-wounded Lamb,
> Saying, 'Ah, remember me, that am
> Italia.' (From deep sea to sea
> Earth heard, earth knew her, that this was she.)
> '*Ricorditi.*'

> (*PS* ii. 167)

Yet, while Christ's sufferings are seen as purposeless, being exploited by others for their own ends, Italy is seen as a figure of innate strength and more deserving of sympathy in that her brave sufferings inspire action and loyalty: 'Give us thy light, thy might, thy love' (*PS* i. 168). St Catherine of Siena, the other dominant female type in the poem, is also seen as an example of effective power and agency as she was led by sympathy to action. The historical Catherine (1347–80) began her spiritual life in prayer and meditation, but turned to wider public affairs when, in 1375, seeking mediation in the armed conflict between Florence, other communes and the papal government, she journeyed to Avignon, where she successfully persuaded Pope Gregory XI to leave France and return to Rome, thus restoring peace to her country:

> Then in her sacred saving hands
> She took the sorrows of the lands,
> With maiden palms she lifted up
> The sick time's blood-embittered cup,
> And in her virgin garment furled
> The faint limbs of the wounded world.
> Clothed with calm love and clear desire,
> She went forth in her soul's attire
> A missive fire.
>
> (*PS* ii. 162)

Swinburne portrays Catherine as a patriot and a visionary. In her own time, as he points out in an explanatory note, the Pope was 'the living symbol of Italian hope and unity', and thus he implies that, by seeking him out and bringing him back to Italy, Catherine's actions foreshadow those of later generations whose goal is Italian unification. St Catherine becomes a prototype of the woman activist and, in his note, Swinburne praises her 'solid and actual qualities which insure to her no ignoble place on the noble roll of Italian women who have deserved well of Italy' (*PS* ii. 238).

Swinburne's use of feminine types receives its most signal treatment in 'Hertha', the centrepiece of *Songs before Sunrise*, the poem that Swinburne thought his best (20 Feb. 1875; *Letters*, iii. 15). Hertha, who takes her name from a Teutonic earth-goddess, is the All-Mother, the creative principle and life force that energizes matter and motivates the soul. Unlike the Judeo-Christian God and other deities whom she precedes and reduces to mere ciphers, Hertha declares that she does not require man's belief or worship:

I bid you but be;
  I have need not of prayer;
I have need of you free
  As your mouths of mine air;
That my heart may be greater within me, beholding the fruits
  of me fair.

(*PS* ii. 78)

Although Hertha as the principle of growth allows for evil as well as good, the 'Freedom of soul' she desires for her children tends towards the production of democratic, libertarian and republican values: 'love, the beloved Republic, that feeds upon freedom and lives' (*PS* ii. 79). This permissive motherhood is in sharp distinction to the tyrannical constraints of organized religion. One of the most notorious poems in *Songs before Sunrise* is 'Before a Crucifix', an indictment of organized Christianity. The germ of this poem can be found in 'Siena', where the ideals and values of the tortured Christ are corrupted by his church; however, here the narrator's address to the image of the suffering Christ is far more scathing and acrimonious. In the opening of the poem Swinburne's narrator shows downtrodden peasants making a consolatory identification with the image of the tortured Christ, but he insists that the sympathy they are encouraged to find in the image is of little value. Institutionalized by the Church, the crucifix that portrays Christ's suffering is seen as endorsing rather than aiding or challenging the suffering of the poor and oppressed. As a body, the 'People', the poor, are themselves crucified by their oppressors. The humanity that Christ possessed while he lived is betrayed by 'blood-blackened altars' and 'the poison of the crucifix'. In sum, the image of the crucified Christ contrasts unfavourably with Swinburne's inspiring female images of suffering and strength. The poem ends with the narrator telling the image on the crucifix that, if he is so diminished as to be only the impotent figurehead of establishment Christianity, then he should 'Come down, be done with, cease give o'er; / Hide thyself, strive not, be no more' (*PS* ii. 87). While the sentiments of Swinburne's poem would nowadays strike a chord with liberal Christians objecting to the institutionalized exploitation and dilution of Christ's message, on publication the poem unsurprisingly caused great offence because of its perceived blasphemy. In Marie Corelli's bestselling novel of 1895 *The Sorrows of Satan*, the poem is denounced as corrupting the morality of Lady Sibyl Elton, one of the principal female characters.[17] Like its partner poem 'Christmas Antiphones', 'Before a Crucifix' is influenced by Mazzini's anti-clericalism. However, Mazzini himself was a great admirer of Christ's teachings, and, under his influence, Swinburne, as he later told his sister Isabel (*Letters*, vi. 168), started to reread the Gospels with renewed appreciation. Although he never abandoned his anti-theism, there is some evidence that in later life he regretted the perceived insult of his verses to the person of Christ.[18]

After *Songs before Sunrise*, Swinburne, in spite of the increasing debility caused by his alcoholic episodes, enjoyed a substantial period of creative productivity. In 1874 he brought out the formidably voluminous *Bothwell*, the successor to *Chastelard* (1865) and the second of his three plays that explore the life and loves of Mary, Queen of Scots. Another political collection, *Songs of Two Nations*, which included the 1867 'Song of Italy', was published in 1875. This collection reprinted the controversial 'Diræ', a sonnet sequence previously published in *The Examiner* in 1873, which vilified Swinburne's *bête noire*, Napoleon III, who had died in exile earlier that same year at Chislehurst, Kent. The year 1875 also saw the publication of *Essays and Studies*, which collected many of Swinburne's best articles to date, including, in addition to essays on the artworks in the Uffizi and Royal Academy, discriminating estimates of Coleridge, Byron, Matthew Arnold, Dante Gabriel Rossetti and William Morris. Swinburne's third publication in this year was his innovative study of the Elizabethan playwright George Chapman, which also includes a spirited defence of the poetry of Robert Browning, which Swinburne had admired since his time at Oxford. *Erectheus*, Swinburne's classical verse drama, appeared the following year in 1876. Written partly to rebut those of his critics who had complained that *Atalanta in Calydon* (1865) had not adhered strongly enough to Greek dramatic models, the play rigorously follows the classical conventions. More austere than its predecessor, it nonetheless also makes its female characters central, the lead protagonists being Chthonia, virgin daughter of Erectheus, King of Athens, and her mother Praxithea. After they have discovered that Chthonia's death is required as a sacrifice to avert the destruction of Athens, the nobly resigned young woman and her grieving mother enact a female passion play, reviving the nationalist types of heroic female suffering and sacrifice seen in *Songs before Sunrise*. In 1877 Swinburne published his book *A Note on Charlotte Brontë*, which made clear his preference for Brontë's novels over those of George Eliot and also indicated his admiration for Emily Brontë, whom he would praise in subsequent essays. His epistolary novel *A Year's Letters* was also serialized in *The Tatler* under the facetious pseudonym of Mrs Horace Manners. The next year he published a second collection *Poems and Ballads Series 2*, a volume that introduces another new note into his writing.

POEMS AND BALLADS 2 (1878)

Poems and Ballads 2, dedicated to his friend the explorer Richard Burton, shares many characteristics with Swinburne's previous collections such as experimentation with complex verse forms and metres and homage to various literary and other figures. The French writers François Villon, Victor Hugo, Charles Baudelaire, Théophile Gautier all receive specific tributes, while 'In the Bay' celebrates Marlowe and Shelley, along with other Elizabethan dramatists. Cardinal Newman and Thomas Carlyle are praised with some reservations in 'The Two Leaders'. The political note of *Songs before Sunrise* is much diminished but still sounds (though in a more jingoistic spirit) in 'The White Czar', and 'Rizpah', which inveigh against Russia, and in a sonnet for the exiled revolutionary and president of the short-lived Hungarian republic, Louis Kossuth (1802–94). Giordano Bruno, the Renaissance rationalist philosopher, executed for his heretical views, is commemorated in a two-sonnet poem that views him as a secular and humanist martyr and inspirational free-thinker. 'The Last Oracle', the poem that opens the volume, continues Swinburne's quarrel with Christianity and revisits the religious and philosophical myth-making seen in 'Hertha'. Like the earlier 'Hymn to

69

Proserpine', 'The Last Oracle' laments the defeat of the pagan deities by Christianity, but goes on 'to reinvoke Apollo to reappear in these days when the Galilean too is conquered and Christ has followed Pan to death'. Apollo in this poem represents 'the inner sunlight of thought or imagination and the gift of speech and song whence all Gods or ideas of Gods possible to man take form and fashion' (8 Feb. 1876; *Letters*, iii. 137). Swinburne's facility as a translator, apparent in *Poems and Ballads 1*, now comes to the fore in his excellent much-admired translations of the ballads of the late-medieval poet François Villon and in the sentimental poem 'From Victor Hugo'. His ease with other languages is also evident in the verses that end the volume: the sestina in French, 'Nocturne', which he wrote at Mallarmé's request for the journal *La République des lettres*, the poems (two in French and one in Latin) memorializing Théophile Gautier, and the Latin address 'Ad Catullum'.

As already indicated, many of the tribute poems of *Poems and Ballads 2* are elegies.[19] The most deservedly famous of these is the majestic 'Ave Atque Vale' written in honour of Baudelaire, one of the earliest poems in the collection, which was written in May 1867 in response to a premature report of Baudelaire's death, and, after the poet's eventual decease in August, published in the *Fortnightly Review* in January 1868. However, the volume also contains the elegant 'Memorial Verses on the Death of Théophile Gautier' in addition to the elegies in French and Latin already mentioned. Two poems commemorate the poet Bryan Proctor, known as 'Barry Cornwall', who had died in 1874 aged 87, and another, 'Epicede', the American consul in Florence (formerly United States consul-general for Italy), James Lorimer Graham, who died in 1876. A more personal note is struck in 'Inferiæ', a poem written for the poet's father Admiral Swinburne who died on 4 March 1877. This emphasis on death is counterpointed but scarcely outweighed by 'A Birth-Song', written to announce the arrival of William Michael Rossetti's baby daughter, Olivia, in September 1875. The named elegies of *Poems and Ballads 2*, distinguished though some of them are, are not the most truly representative poems of this volume. The elegiac note, which is characteristic of the volume as a whole, enters into a range of poems where it is mediated by a more personal and reflective lyricism. This wistful lyricism, heard occasionally in *Poems and Ballads 1* though less evident in the more public and polemical verse of *Songs before Sunrise*, informs some of the most beautiful verse of *Poems and Ballads 2*: 'A Forsaken Garden', 'The Year of the Rose', 'Sestina', 'A Ballad of Dreamland', 'Four Songs of Four Seasons', 'Relics', and 'A Vision of Spring in Winter'. The volume is pervaded by the sense of regret and nostalgia. The themes of change and transience, so marked in *Poems and Ballads 1*, are revisited but here the emphasis is on memory, and often, irretrievable loss. More intimate in tone than *Poems and Ballads 1*, there is also a strong sense of reserve and secrecy in many of these poems, as the speaker keeps private, or holds in reserve, the true source of his hopes and fears. Flowers, especially roses, are the dominant motif, and the fading of flowers and, less frequently, their regeneration become symbols of the passing and occasional revival of memories, hopes, desires. Such poems in themselves seem like early flowerings of Symbolism, and it is certainly easy to see how a number of these dreamlike or trancelike poems anticipate Yeats's early poetry with its love of roses and its attempts to induce, through rhythm, mesmeric dream states 'in which the mind liberated from the pressure of the will is unfolded in symbols'. Georges Lafourcade would also write of these poems: 'Never was perhaps the art of Swinburne so closely akin to music, so elusive of translation, and yet, in a way, so perfect. ... Swinburne's elaborate rhythms are generally meant to create in the mind of the reader a neutral state which is neither joy nor sorrow, waking nor sleeping, yet is tinged with dreamy melancholy.'[20]

One of the most important of these poems is 'Relics' (*PS* iii. 26–8), originally published as 'North and South' in the *Fortnightly Review* for May 1873.[21] Swinburne had some difficulty in naming this poem, which he first refers to as the 'Two Flowers' (*Letters*, ii. 238), commenting in a later letter to John Morley, editor of *Fortnightly*, 'the *names* of the flowers would make far too ponderous and polysyllabic a title for anything under a South Sea Idyl or epic' (*Letters*, ii. 240). The two flowers mentioned in the poem are, respectively, the white laurustine, which represents the North, or England, and the white acacia, which represents Italy, the South. The flowers also evoke specific places: in the case of the first, it is the West Undercliff of the Isle of Wight, a verdant and scenic platform of land facing the sea, backed by tall, thickly wooded slopes, which stretches from Bonchurch to Blackgang Chine, a distance of about six miles. The Isle of Wight was the location of Swinburne's boyhood home, East Dene, Bonchurch, situated in the Undercliff, and his uncle Sir Henry Percy Gordon (father of Mary Gordon, the woman generally supposed to be Swinburne's 'lost love'), owned a house known as The Orchard, at Niton, which had a beautiful garden, and commanded views of nearly the whole of the West Undercliff. Laurustine is known to have flourished close by this house.[22] On 4 June 1884, concerning 'Relics', Swinburne wrote to the writer and traveller May Crommelin, who wished to include some extracts from his verse on flowers in an anthology: 'I think with you the laurustinus one of the most delightful flowers of shrubs of its kind. You would have admired the long close range of them above the Channel which suggested my tribute' (*Letters*, v. 70). The second flower, the white acacia, evokes the slopes outside the city walls of San Gimignano, near Siena. This well-preserved medieval town, visited by Swinburne in the spring of 1864, is famous for its thirteen towers and, among other treasures, its chapel of Santa Fina in the Collegiata, decorated by Ghirlandaio. Swinburne evidently admired the blossom of the acacias, seeing them as typifying the place; indeed, a local wine, Vernaccia di San Gimignano, is said to have a bouquet that is reminiscent of the scent of acacias. Another poem, 'Spring in Tuscany', in 'Four Songs of Four Seasons', which mentions San Gimignano, also celebrates acacias. In 'Relics' the uplifting marvel of the Tuscan spring is perhaps enhanced by the allusion, in stanza fifteen, to the flower-like Santa Fina, whose great sanctity caused the room in which she died to be miraculously filled with blooms and fragrance, violets to spring from the board on which she had lain, and wallflowers to spring from a nearby village tower.

Swinburne loved flowers, and the luminosity of white blooms seems to have had a special attraction for him. The Irish writer Coulson Kernahan described the poet's 'ecstasy of delight' when he presented him with a bouquet of arum lilies, lilies of the valley and snowdrops, commenting: 'A flower had been to him ... the one unchanging and perfect thing in a changing and decaying world, as fair, as fresh, and as immortal as in the days of our youth.'[23] Such a view seems paradoxical, for a flower is apparently among the most transient and ephemeral of things, and yet, in the lasting impression of its untainted and spontaneous beauty and in its potential to renew itself each year, the flower, like memory, can be seen to outlast many other things deemed more enduring. A lover of Blake, Swinburne may also have recalled 'Auguries of Innocence' with its lines about seeing 'a Heaven in a Wild Flower' and holding 'Infinity in the palm of your hand'. These transcendent qualities are surely central to 'Relics', where the living flowers of the present moment are seen to conjure up their predecessors. The flowers of 'Relics' are assumed by Ross C. Murfin to be pressed flowers, but it seems important to me that they are vital blooms, perhaps given as part of a bouquet or plucked in an upper-class garden or conservatory – Swinburne sent the poem to Morley from his family home, Holmwood, Oxfordshire, in early April 1873 – for they possess fragrance and the acacia blossom is described as 'tender', 'soft' and 'overblown', words that seem inappropriate for a dried pressed flower.[24] It is these living flowers, which then summon up reminiscences of their forebears, that grew *en masse* in two places dear to the speaker's remembrance and are associated by him with particular memories.

Written in April, the month of his own birthday, 'Relics' evokes spring, Swinburne's favourite season, and in particular the 'lost Aprils' and the 'lost Mays' of bygone years. It is the perfume of the white laurustine, a member of the sweetly scented viburnum family – 'This flower that smells of honey and the sea' – that acts as a cue to memory and launches the poem (anticipating Proust's famous treatment of mnemonic sense impressions by forty years). Notably the flowers of the laurustine are masculinized ('brethren', 'Live sons') as the speaker stresses their vigour, tenacity and hardiness as they endure their exposure to the sea and elements. This masculinity contrasts with the acacia flower in the second part of the poem, which, although less explicitly so, seems feminine, being exotic, 'tender' and 'soft'. But one suspects that the masculinized laurustine flowers may also stand in for the speaker

73

himself, remembering a time as a boy or youth when he too enjoyed the spirited, carefree, out-of-doors play in all weathers, of the kind we know Swinburne enjoyed when he rode, swam in the sea and climbed the cliffs of his island home. These animated flowers seem to take the same robust pleasure in sea and elements that a free-spirited boy might take – 'Their hearts were glad of the free place's glory' – and indeed their comparison to 'things born of the sea and the bright day' looks ahead to the semi-autobiographical 'Thalassius' (1880) in which the young poet is the child of Apollo and a sea-nymph. However, towards the end of this section, a romantic, even erotic note enters the poem, for the smell of the laurustine flowers 'A keen-edged odour of the sun and showers / Was as the smell of fresh honeycomb / Made sweet for mouths of none but paramours'. This sensual detail, which presents the sweet breath of the flower as something to be consumed and savoured by a lover, irresistibly provokes thoughts of shared kisses, suggesting that first love is also associated with the memories of the flowers and their locale.

Turning then to the more fragile acacia flower, which evokes Italy, the speaker asks: 'Where once thou grew, what else for me grew there?' The answer is love, which seems to have flourished, as the flower does, during a spring spent in Italy. However, the fragrance of the flower now reminds him of that love's failure, which came after a period of hope and idealism. Through the subtly eroticized image of the flower 'That for the sun's love makes its bosom wide / At sunrise', the speaker intimates how the flower symbolized his ardent youthful desire and hope for the future, while he was still unwitting of the disappointment to come. He recalls a visit to San Gimignano, where the acacias blossomed on the slopes around the city. The memory of the noble flower-clad trees – 'How king-like they stood up into the day' – seems to intimate the confident sense of resolve and promise that he felt at this time. 'Such words of message have dead flowers to say,' comments the speaker, referring to these recollections, although it is hard to catch his precise tone – sad, rueful, resigned, worldly-wise? – or to understand quite what he reads in the message. The last stanza pictures him preparing to throw both flowers away and thereby end both his train of thought and the poem, and, as he does so, he teases the reader with a question: 'Before I throw them and these flowers away, / Who knows but I what memories too take flight?'

We can somewhat disturb the tantalizing yet moving privacy of this declaration with a biographical reading of the poem, which would connect these experiences of love to Swinburne's thwarted feelings for his cousin Mary Gordon, who most likely announced her engagement to Colonel Robert Disney Leith in the second part of 1864, after Swinburne had returned from his trip to Italy. (The couple married in June 1865.) The line 'dreams now dwelling where dead roses dwell' links the poem with 'A Forsaken Garden', which also has an Isle of Wight setting, and treats love and transience through the image of a decayed rose garden.[25] Certainly in later life Swinburne had misgivings about revisiting scenes that had held significance for him. In 1873, shortly after he had written 'Relics', he wrote to friends that his family wanted him to accompany them on a summer vacation to stay at 'a place of my uncle Henry Gordon's in the Isle of Wight' (*Letters*, ii. 254), presumably The Orchard. Swinburne had not visited since the family had left the island in 1865, and it is evident that the prospective trip generated some anxieties: 'I may as well once for all break through all sentiment of reluctance and association and tread out all sense of old pain and pleasure for ever, if I can, by coming back in this my old age to where I was so happy and unhappy as a child and youth' (*Letters*, ii. 251). In fact he does not seem to have undertaken the trip, leaving it until the following summer of 1874, when he appears to have come to terms with the past and enjoyed a long productive stay at The Orchard, reading, writing and swimming daily. However, after 1864, his strong political interests notwithstanding, he never revisited Italy, affectionately described in 'Relics' as 'that one land of ours'. It is probable that his disappointed hopes for an Italian republic also colour the poem. The younger man of 1864 innocently and almost unconsciously sees the 'fair brave trees' of San Gimignano as embodying republican freedom and strength – each of them democratically becomes 'king-like' in its own right – while the idealistic but swift-fading 'thoughts', 'loves' and 'dreams' of stanza twelve may also relate to political enthusiasms that meet with disillusion. So, too, the 'sunrise' of stanza thirteen, which additionally represents the glorious dawn of republican expectation, fails to fulfil its promise, a disappointment that retrospectively casts its shadow over the poet's own *Songs before Sunrise*.

However, whether one chooses to read these biographical details into the poem or not, one cannot fail to notice the way in which the speaker skilfully uses the flowers to mediate the boundaries between his present and past selves, between states of innocence and experience. He does not confuse these states, but manages to inhabit and recapture his original idealism without any latter-day sense of superiority, while at the same time retaining the sad vantage point of hindsight. The complex mixed emotional tenor of the poem, its sweetness and sadness, is based on this poignant disjunction, which is also a temporary conjunction. Lyric typically mingles pain with pleasure, and Swinburne's lyricism in this poem and in other of the verses of *Poems and Ballads 2*, continues to extend readerly sympathy by drawing it into these exquisitely subtle and painful emotional combinations. In 'Relics' the emotional complexity generated by revisiting the past is beautifully enhanced by poetic form. Swinburne uses the Rubáiyát stanza, which he borrowed from Edward FitzGerald's translation of Omar Kháyyám and first used in 'Laus Veneris', so the form is itself a 'relic' of both 'ancient' poetry and his own early poem. However, he innovates upon the rhyme scheme of the Rubáiyát stanza (*aaba*) so that the third line of each stanza rhymes with the first, second and fourth lines of the following stanza (*aaba, bbcb, ccdc*, etc.). Thus each stanza perpetually retains an echo or 'relic' of the stanza before, hearkening back to or rewakening after a slight pause or interval the reminiscence of something just gone by. The following example illustrates this, but the effect is also strengthened here by the deliberate repetition of the phrase 'dead memory', literally 'revived' from one stanza to another across the white space separating them:

> A star out of the skies love used to know
> Here held in hand, a stray left yet to show
>   What flowers my heart was full of in the days
> That are long since gone down dead memory's flow.

Dead memory that revives on doubtful ways,
Half hearkening what the buried season says
    Out of the world of the unapparent dead
Where the lost Aprils are, and the lost Mays.

(PS iii. 26)

'Relics' proves itself to be an influential poem about memory, in that it echoes in at least two later nineteenth-century poems. In 'Tuberoses' (1888), a trio of sonnets by A. Mary F. Robinson, the speaker sadly observes that the fragrant white flower given her by her lover is already fading, a perception that leads her into a meditation on transience in which she notes that only art, dreams and thoughts, even if delusive, last. In 'White Heliotrope' (1895), Arthur Symons's self-consciously 'modern' speaker describes a bedroom scene after a sexual encounter with a woman, probably a prostitute, and casually remarks that the scene 'Will rise, a ghost of memory', if ever again his 'handkerchief / Is scented with white heliotrope.' Symons's deliberately anti-romantic poem aggressively cuts against its Swinburneian precursor and the poignant sentiments of reminiscence. But, skilful though the poem is, the air of sophisticated insouciance affected by its male speaker can seem rather smug and thin, especially when set alongside the densely layered emotions of 'Relics'.

The other major poem of nostalgia from *Poems and Ballads 2* that I wish to discuss is 'A Vision of Spring in Winter' (*PS* iii. 94–7), in which the speaker, yearning for springtime in the depths of winter, 'the pale time of the flowerless rose', imagines 'The ghost arisen of May before the May', the 'girl-child spring' revitalizing nature. Time relations in this poem are complex. As in 'Relics', memory crosses the boundary into the past, but, simultaneously, desire disrupts futurity, taking the season-to-come out of time. The speaker imagines the future spring brought into the present moment – 'I stretch my heart out toward the springtime lands, / I stretch my spirit forth to the fair hours' – while recalling the recent past spring – 'I send my love back to the lovely time.' 'Ghost' in this poem predominantly refers to the shape of things to come, although it also retains its more usual reference to the image of that which has passed; for the cycle of the year means that every spring is itself a revival of previous springs, the new season always a repetition, reflection or ghost of those gone by.

That sense of echo or repetition is also strongly enhanced by the poem's subtle evocation of Romanticism. Swinburne rated Keats 'next to Shakespeare ... as a flower-singer' (*Letters*, v. 122), and evocations of Keats, the odes especially, are omnipresent in the sensitivity to natural beauty, the extreme smoothness and suaveness of the language – 'Sweet foot of spring which with her footfall sows / Late snowlike flowery leavings of the snows' – and in direct allusions such as the 'tender-coloured night', which rewrites 'Tender is the night' of 'To a Nightingale'. The personification of 'the maid, the girl-child spring' reminds us of the allegorical maidens of the 'Ode on Indolence' and the graceful figure of Autumn in 'To Autumn'; the vision of absent spring evokes the envisioning of invisible flowers in 'To a Nightingale'; and the unanswerable questions addressed to the spring in the second of Swinburne's stanzas – 'What sleep enchants thee? what delight deceives?' – recall the fruitless questioning of the Grecian urn – 'What mad pursuit? what struggle to escape?' And yet, perhaps it is Shelley to whom the poem owes more in actual sentiment. His unfinished poem of 1822, 'The Zucca', opens with the lines 'Summer was dead and Autumn was expiring, / And infant Winter laughed upon the land / All cloudlessly and cold'. Shelley's speaker mourns the decay of beauty, hungering after an elusive spirit of vitality that dwells in all things. Having found a neglected Zucca plant abandoned by the riverside, he takes it home and nurses it back into health, feeding it with his tears so that it grows beautiful and strong. While Swinburne's speaker lacks the histrionic morbidity of Shelley's narrator, the poem shares the central image of a midwinter revivification generated by a desire for lost beauty.

In imagining the ghost of spring as a young girl, Swinburne identifies, as he frequently does in his poetry, imaginative and natural energy with the feminine, though here it is a more gentle presence. He draws perhaps on Shelley's poem 'The Sensitive Plant', where the 'Power' that tends the garden is feminine and the flowers 'felt the spirit that came / From her glowing fingers through all their frame'. Swinburne's own 'girl-child spring' also carries out her duties with a light touch as she 'kindles with her mouth's own colouring / The fearful firstlings of the plumeless boughs'. However, she is still insuperable, and the speaker celebrates her forthcoming triumph over winter – 'thy maiden breath / Shall put at last the deadly days to death'. Yet he also understands that, although spring returns, his own youth will not – 'those first fair years / Whose flowers revive not with thy flowers on earth'. In the final two stanzas he calmly declares that he does not expect spring to restore to him any of the gifts or pleasures of youth. Alluding again perhaps to *Songs before Sunrise* in the image of 'youth' who 'Sang towards the sun that was to crown his head', he recalls his loves, aspirations and ideals, 'the hopes that triumphed and fell dead, / The sweet swift eyes and songs of hours that were', and resigns himself to the fact that they are buried 'deeper than the sea'. It is the physical presence only of spring that can come back to him: 'flowers ... and winds, and hours of ease'. Thus the spring 'all its April to the world thou mayst / Give back, and half my April back to me'. The sweet modulations of this poem act like a self-administered salve that soothes but cannot obliterate the underlying pain. The longed-for vision of spring promises to cancel out the negations of winter, but, once it is achieved, the speaker realizes that it cannot make good his own deeper losses, which he then bravely confronts. Coming to terms with the subtractions exacted from him by time, he accepts the reality of what the spring can give – sensuous pleasure but not the hopes and opportunities it once offered him. Yet, even while we are made to feel keenly the diminishment of the speaker's April, the poem's perfect music and consummate form release their own enchantment, reminding us of the productive age-old connection between pain and creativity. Ultimately there is more that is restorative about this poem than gets said in that it enacts a lyric paradigm turning loss into melody. The painful pleasure of the poem is that it indirectly speaks to every reader's inevitable losses, allowing something of that existential smart to penetrate through its protective sweetness in a way that only heightens both perceptions.

It has been customary to regard this poem, written in 1875 when Swinburne was at a low ebb, as intimating the onset of a creative winter.[26] Such a view is dramatically wide of the mark. In addition to some of the critical works mentioned in the opening to Chapter 3, the three volumes published in 1880 each contain work of high value. 'Thalassius' and 'On the Cliffs' distinguish *Songs of the Springtides*, *The Heptalogia* is a dazzling collection of parodies of Swinburne's poetic contemporaries, while *Studies in Song* contains two important landscape poems 'Evening on the Broads' and 'By the North Sea', the last recently evoked by the late W. G. Sebald in his idiosyncratic East Anglian travelogue *The Rings of Saturn* (1998). Most importantly of all, Swinburne still had ahead of him the completion and publication of his masterly epic *Tristram of Lyonesse* (1882), a work I shall return to in the coda to this volume.

3

Swinburne's Aesthetic Prose

While best known for his poetry, Swinburne was also a skilled and influential writer of prose. His prose publications span a period from 1862 to 1908 and include essays on art, poetry, fiction and drama and a number of pieces that defend his own writings and critical views. They also include the brilliant epistolary novel *A Year's Letters*, written mainly during 1862, published pseudonymously as a serial in *The Tatler* in 1877, and republished under Swinburne's own name as *Love's Cross-Currents* in 1905.[1] The unfinished and somewhat fragmentary novel *Lesbia Brandon*, written between 1864 and 1866, was published posthumously in 1952, sending the entranced poet H.D. 'into an electric coma' (Rooksby, 4). Unrivalled in Britain in his knowledge of French literature, Swinburne produced the first English review of Baudelaire's poetry (1862) and, in an otherwise laudatory essay on Matthew Arnold (1867), tartly pointed out Arnold's deficiencies as a critic of French verse. He also published numerous essays on his idol Victor Hugo, a due proportion of which were reprinted in *A Study of Victor Hugo* (1886). Swinburne's critical impact on English letters was substantial and wide-ranging. He brought out the first book-length literary-critical work on William Blake (1868), which included a ground-breaking appraisal of the 'Prophetic Books' (previously thought unintelligible), made some significant contributions in the newly emergent field of Shakespeare scholarship, and published valuable studies of Elizabethan and seventeenth-century dramatists (John Ford, George Chapman, Ben Jonson, Thomas Middleton and many others) at a time when such writers were still not much read or appreciated. Similarly he did much to boost and consolidate the reputations of Charlotte and Emily Brontë, while an essay of 1902 championed Dickens when his critical fortunes were at a low ebb.

This chapter takes as its focus a number of Swinburne's essays written between 1862 and 1871 in which he virtually pioneered the style of English prose known as 'aesthetic', a style that endeavours to communicate to the reader through evocative description the writer's personal impressions or perceptions of an art object or literary text. Swinburne's early prose is the key influence on Walter Pater, the most important writer of aesthetic prose in the nineteenth century. After Pater's *Studies in the History of the Renaissance* (published on 1 March 1873) had been reviewed approvingly by John Morley, editor of the *Fortnightly Review*, Swinburne, who was among those sent a presentation copy, subsequently told Morley that, when he had praised some of the essays that had earlier been printed in the *Fortnightly*, Pater had replied that he 'considered them as owing their inspiration entirely to the example of my own work in the same line' (11 Apr. 1873; *Letters*, ii. 240). Perfected by Pater, the aesthetic style would be taken up with diverse variations by a whole host of late-nineteenth-century writers who followed. Widely used by the male writers of the *fin de siècle* – a group that includes Oscar Wilde, Arthur Symons, Max Beerbohm and W. B. Yeats – it can also be seen informing the prose of notable women writers such as Vernon Lee, Alice Meynell and Charlotte Mew.

This consideration of Swinburne's prose begins with a brief discussion of two writers who were an influence on him. It then broadens into an examination of three major essays – 'Charles Baudelaire: *Les Fleurs du mal*' (1862), 'The Poems of Dante Gabriel Rossetti' (1870) and 'Simeon Solomon: Notes on his "Vision of Love" and Other Studies' (1871) – that stresses the major linked themes and images of Swinburne's aesthetic criticism and indicates which of his key ideas and images will be absorbed by Pater. In concluding it speculates on the reasons why Swinburne's prose style began to change in the early 1870s.

INFLUENCES

Behind Swinburne's aesthetic prose style lie a number of possible influences of which I shall single out two – one French, one English. The first is the French writer, critic and poet Théophile Gautier (1811–72), the vivid pictorialism of whose fiction and art criticism made a determinable impact on Swinburne, who was reading Gautier in the early 1860s and had an intimate acquaintance with his work, as shown in the fine memorial verses he wrote for him in *Poems and Ballads* 2 (1878). Swinburne was undoubtedly drawn to Gautier's celebrated verbal portraits of beautiful and alluring women, to those *femmes fatales* who exert such an uncannily penetrating gaze. In one of Gautier's most famous stories, 'La Morte amoureuse' (1836), the narrator tells how the vampirical heroine's black brows

> admirably relieved the effect of the sea-green eyes of unsustainable vivacity and brilliancy. What eyes! with a single flash they could have decided a man's destiny: they had a life, a limpidity, an ardor, a humid light which I have never seen in human eyes; – they shot forth rays like arrows, which I could distinctly *see* enter my heart. I know not if the fire which illumined them came from heaven or from hell; but assuredly it came from one or the other. The woman was either an angel or a demon, perhaps both: assuredly she never sprang from the flank of Eve, our common mother.[2]

This fascination with a woman's eyes and her mesmerizing gaze is mirrored by Swinburne, who, for example, in *Lesbia Brandon* devotes nearly a page to the description of Lady Wariston's eyes, of which the following is only a sample:

> These eyes were not hard or shadowless; their colour was full of small soft intricacies of shade and varieties of tone; they could darken with delicate alteration and lighten with splendid change. This iris had fine fibres of light and tender notes of colour that gave the effect of shadow; as if the painter's touch when about to darken the clear fierce beauty of their vital and sensitive gold had paused in time and left them perfect. The pupil was not over large, and seemed as the light touched it of molten purple or of black velvet. (*LB* 1)

That last sentence sounds as if it might have been inspired by Gautier's description of his favourite painting, the *Mona Lisa*, in his essay 'Leonardo da Vinci' (1858), where he notes how the woman's

> sagacious, deep, velvety glance, full of promise, irresistibly entrances and intoxicates, while the sinuous, serpentine mouth, turned up at the corners in a violet penumbra, rallies and with such gentleness, grace, and superiority, that one feels as timid as a school-boy in the presence of a duchess.[3]

Gautier's extensive art criticism, notable for its passages of impressionistic description, had been published in the French press from the 1830s onwards. His 'The Amateur's Guide for the Museum of the Louvre', written for the *Paris Guide* of 1867, is a likely influence on Swinburne's 'Notes on some Pictures of 1868', a commentary on the Royal Academy Exhibition, and his 'Notes on the Designs of the Old Masters at Florence', also published in 1868. In this last essay Swinburne states he is writing up notes taken during an exploration of the Uffizi in the spring of 1864, but he may well have been prompted to do this by the recent appearance of Gautier's 'Guide'. In his 'Guide' Gautier returns to the subject of the *Mona Lisa*, recalling a passage he wrote in 1855 that illustrates how his feminine ideals appear to transcend common humanity:

> From what planet fell into the midst of this azure landscape that strange being with its glance full of the promise of unknown voluptuousness and its divinely ironical expression? ... What troublous fixity in the dark eyes, what a supreme sardonic touch on the lips formed like Cupid's bow! Does it not seem as though La Gioconda were the Isis of a mystic religion, who, believing herself alone, draws aside the folds of her veil, careless whether the imprudent man who should surprise her should go mad and die? Never did the ideal of woman assume a more irresistibly seductive form.[4]

This tendency to divinize or to bestow on pictured women mythic antecedents or analogues is taken up by Swinburne, and Pater after him. However, Gautier and Swinburne use these mythic references to make their women both sinister and, unlike Pater, overtly sexually alluring. A famous passage in Swinburne's 'Notes on the Designs of the Old Masters at

Florence' thus intensifies the sexual menace of a woman wearing a serpentine headdress and body ornaments in a drawing by Michelangelo:

> Her eyes are full of proud and passionless lust after gold and blood; her hair, close and curled, seems ready to shudder in sunder and divide into snakes. Her throat, full and fresh, round and hard to the eye as her bosom and arms, is erect and stately, the head set firm on it without any droop or lift of the chin; her mouth crueller than a tiger's, colder than a snake's, and beautiful beyond a woman's. She is the deadlier Venus incarnate . . . (*SAC* 127; *ES* 319–20)

Just as La Gioconda is Isis, so Michelangelo's snake woman is Venus; and the sexual magnetism of Gautier's Mona Lisa finds a parallel in the lazy seductiveness of Dante Gabriel Rossetti's *Lady Lilith*, as described by Swinburne in 'Notes on Some Pictures of 1868':

> Clothed in soft white garments, she draws out through a comb the heavy mass of hair like thick spun gold to fullest length; her head leans back half sleepily, superb and satiate with its own beauty; the eyes are languid, without love in them or hate; the sweet luxurious mouth has the patience of pleasure fulfilled and complete, the warm repose of passion sure of its delight. . . . Of evil desire or evil impulse she has nothing; and nothing good. She is indifferent, equable, magnetic; she charms and draws down the souls of men by pure force of absorption, in no wise wilful or malignant; outside herself she cannot live, she cannot even see: and because of this she attracts and subdues all men at once in body and in spirit. (*SAC* 132; *ES* 375–6)

Usually remembered for his voluptuous verbal portraits of *femme fatales* such as Rossetti's Lady Lilith or Michelangelo's snake woman, Swinburne was also attracted to images portraying women of a more wistful beauty. This leads us on to the second dominant influence on his prose. A passionate admirer of Shelley, Swinburne would have known well the description of the portrait of Beatrice Cenci in the preface to *The Cenci* (1820):

> There is a fixed and pale composure upon the features: she seems sad and stricken down in spirit, yet the despair thus expressed is lightened by the patience of gentleness. Her hair is bound with

folds of white drapery from which the yellow strings of her golden hair escape, and fall about her neck. The moulding of her face is exquisitely delicate; the eye brows are distinct and arched: the lips have that permanent meaning of imagination and sensibility which suffering has not repressed and which it seems as if death scarcely could extinguish.[5]

This passage of Shelley's is important in that it contains a number of the keynotes that will sound in Swinburne's aesthetic writing. It makes the face of a beautiful woman the focus of attention and uses that face to evoke mood and complex emotion. The concentration on the poignant arresting gaze, the indelible marks of sadness and suffering emphasized by alliteration, the elegant balancing of phrases and clauses, and the immediacy of the present tense that involves the reader as a spectator, are all typical of a certain kind of Swinburneian prose portrait. Thus, like Beatrice Cenci a sexual victim, Dante Gabriel Rossetti's *La Pia*, displayed at the Royal Academy exhibition of 1868,

is seen looking forth from the ramparts of her lord's castle, over the fatal lands without; her pallid splendid face hangs a little forward, wan and white against the mass of dark deep hair; under her hands is a work of embroidery, hanging still on the frame unfinished; just touched by the weak weary hands, it trails forward across the lap of her pale green raiment, into the foreground of the picture. In her eyes is a strange look of wonder and sorrow and fatigue, without fear and without pain, as though she were even now looking beyond earth and into the soft and sad air of purgatory: she presses the deadly marriage-ring into the flesh of her finger, so deep that the soft skin is bloodless and blanched from the intense imprint of it.   (*SAC* 133–4; *ES* 378)

While they provide a foil to his more sensual female types, Swinburne's melancholy subjects are not necessarily 'pure' women but may have suffered some kind of sexual or amatory disappointment. In his novel *A Year's Letters*, the elusive Amicia, Lady Cheyne, trapped like La Pia in a loveless marriage, sounds as if she has stepped out of one of Rossetti's more poignant paintings. Frank Cheyne, Amicia's lover and cousin, is haunted by

such an invincible exquisite memory of a face ten times more beautiful and loveable to have in sight of one; pale when I saw it last, as if pulled down by its hair, heavily weighted about the eyes with a presage of tears, sealed with sorrow and piteous with an infinite unaccomplished desire. The old deep gold hair and luminous gray-green eyes shot through with colours of sea-water in sunlight and threaded with faint keen lines of fire and light about the pupil ... (*AYL* 130–1)

Swinburne would also have been familiar with the impressionistic descriptions in Shelley's 'Notes on Sculptures in Rome and Florence' written in 1819, some of the most significant of which had been published by Thomas Medwin in 1832–3 and 1847 and by Mary Shelley in 1840.[6] Along with Gautier's 'Guide', Shelley's 'Notes', many of which describe statues in the Uffizi, probably helped inspire Swinburne's 'Notes on the Designs of the Old Masters at Florence' of 1868, which examines paintings in the same gallery. Shelley is particularly sensitive to the expression of the sculptures he views, and one of the 'Notes' published by Medwin details a statue of Minerva, describing its emotional appeal in a way that anticipates a dominant note in Swinburne's aesthetic prose:

Her face, upraised to heaven, is animated with a profound, sweet, and impassioned melancholy, with an earnest, and fervid, and disinterested pleading against some vast and inevitable wrong. It is the joy and poetry of sorrow making grief beautiful, and giving it that nameless feeling which, from the imperfection of language, we call pain, but which is not all pain, though a feeling which makes not only its possessor, but the spectator of it, prefer it to what is called pleasure, in which all is not pleasure.[7]

'CHARLES BAUDELAIRE: *LES FLEURS DU MAL*' (1862)

This note of complex mixed emotion sounds in 'Charles Baudelaire: *Les Fleurs du mal*', Swinburne's first major piece of criticism, which appeared in the *Spectator* on 6 September 1862, where it seems Swinburne uses the poetry of Baudelaire to meditate on and presage the themes and perspectives of his own emergent *Poems and Ballads*. Opening with a spirited claim that 'the art of poetry has absolutely nothing to do with didactic matter at all' (*SAC* 28), Swinburne establishes craftsmanship as the only true criterion for good poetry – 'His perfect workmanship makes every subject admirable and respectable' (*SAC* 28) – before proceeding to evoke the heady exoticism of Baudelaire's collection, which 'has the languid lurid beauty of close and threatening weather – a heavy heated temperature, with dangerous hothouse scents in it; thick shadow of cloud about it, and fire of molten light' (*SAC* 29). Throughout the essay alliteration emphasizes the keynotes, as here again, even more noticeably, 'the sights seen are steeped most often in sad light and sullen colour' (*SAC* 29). One of the most striking things about this review (and one that must have been most surprising to its readership) is the way Swinburne immediately forces a qualitative change in the emotional atmosphere of Victorian literature by championing psychological and moral complexity against the happy certainties of common sense and convention. Writing of *Les Fleurs du mal*, he comments of Baudelaire, 'Throughout the chief part of this book, he has chosen to dwell mainly on sad and strange things – the weariness of pain and the bitterness of pleasure – the perverse happiness and wayward sorrows of exceptional people' (*SAC* 28–9).

Swinburne's use of the word 'strange', a word that will recur repeatedly in his early aesthetic criticism, prefigures Pater's pronouncement in 1876 that 'it is the addition of strangeness to beauty, that constitutes the romantic character in art'.[8] Pater, too, will draw heavily on the word in the essays that make up *Studies in the History of the Renaissance* (1873), a case in point being the essay on Leonardo, first published in 1869. His use of 'strange' and related terms to describe certain artists and their works is nowadays frequently read as a code intimating homosexual tendencies, which was properly legible only to a select group of similarly oriented readers. But to see this as the exclusive meaning of such language, especially in contexts such as the just-cited statement on 'strangeness and beauty', seems unnecessarily reductive. Certainly in Swinburne the use of the word 'strange' has a much wider provenance and tends to describe sexual and other behaviours and characteristics that fall outside the mainstream. Thaïs Morgan has suggested that in his review of Baudelaire Swinburne is constructing for the writer a character of 'masculine androgyny', but, although as a male poet Swinburne was unusually open to feminization, the essay more evidently emphasizes a temperamental sado-masochism that has a much wider philosophical and aesthetic application.[9]

In describing Baudelaire's work, Swinburne is evidently thinking about the character of his own poetry. Baudelaire's work unites or brings together ideas or images that might normally be regarded as discrepant or incongruous, a characteristic reflected in his style in, for example, the celebrated synaesthesia of his sonnet 'Correspondances', arguably an influence on Swinburne's poem 'August', published in the *Spectator* alongside this review. Baudelaire's verse then, appropriately, is praised in synaesthetic terms – 'The sound of his metres suggests colour and perfume' (*SAC* 29) – and indeed this kind of synaesthetic evaluation typifies many of the artists Swinburne praises during the next decade – Baudelaire, Blake, Rossetti, Solomon – all of whom, like Swinburne himself, have strongly synthesizing instincts. In the passage about 'perverse happiness and wayward sorrows', we see, in an authoritative early form, the mixing of categories typical of Swinburneian style and sensibility and the resultant emotional complexity that characterizes poems such as 'Laus Veneris'. Describing Baudelaire's 'Litanies of Satan' as 'one of the noblest lyrics ever written; the sound of it between wailing and triumph, as it were the blast blown by the trumpets of a brave army in irretrievable defeat' (*SAC* 34), Swinburne previews the emotional tenor of his own 'Hymn to Proserpine' (written perhaps about the time of this review), which robustly laments the displacement of paganism and its untroubled pleasures by the austerities of Christianity. A similar strain of regret will also be heard in the second half of 'Dolores'.[10]

Accenting the dark and troubled side of human nature, Swinburne observes of Baudelaire: 'The writer delights in problems, and has a natural leaning to obscure and sorrowful things. Failure and sorrow, next to physical beauty and perfection of sound or scent, seem to have an infinite attraction for him' (*SAC* 29). This notion of the writer as interested in problems is one too easily missed out of descriptions of Swinburne, whose poems, as shown in Chapter 1, precisely tease out the strands of particular problems or crises for investigation. The continuing stress on sorrow allies Swinburne to a markedly European strain of Romanticism, in which what Goethe called 'the worship of sorrow' was held to be one of the characteristics of the Romantic spirit (and something Pater, writing against the grain, would later reinscribe back into certain manifestations of Greek religion).[11] Finally Swinburne makes explicit the strong sadomasochism of Baudelaire: 'Not the luxuries of pleasure in their simple first form, but the sharp and cruel enjoyments of pain, the acrid relish of suffering felt or inflicted, the sides on which nature looks unnatural, go to make up the stuff and substance of this poetry' (*SAC* 30). This quality in Baudelaire is a note that will sound in poems such as 'Anactoria', 'Dolores' and 'Faustine', but Swinburne insists that such complex topics demand the fullest exertion of the literary artist's capabilities: 'Only the supreme excellence of words will suffice to grapple with and fitly render the effects of such material' (*SAC* 30). He again praises Baudelaire's consummate use of form – 'M. Baudelaire's mastery of the sonnet form is worth remarking as a test of his natural bias towards such forms of verse as are most nearly capable of perfection' and 'The main charm of the book is, upon the whole, that nothing is wrongly given, nothing capable of being re-written or improved on its own ground' (*SAC* 30) – reminding us of the finish and craftsmanship that will characterize *Poems and Ballads*.

'THE POEMS OF DANTE GABRIEL ROSSETTI' (1870)

The stress on craftsmanship is continued in the essays that Swinburne produced some years later when he was established as a major new poet. Dante Gabriel Rossetti and Simeon Solomon, both close friends of Swinburne's, are singled out as artists who demonstrate excellence in their use of form. In 'The Poems of Dante Gabriel Rossetti', published in the *Fortnightly Review* in May 1870, and written as a review of Rossetti's *Poems* (1870), Swinburne stipulates that the great poet's work must appear effortlessly flawless:

> There must be an instinct and a resolution of excellence which will allow no shortcoming or malformation of thought or word: there

must be also so natural a sense of right as to make any such deformity or defect impossible, and leave upon the work done no trace of any effort to avoid or achieve. . . . in the best work there must be no trace of a laborious or a languid hand.   (*ES* 62)

Rossetti's poetry is a prime example of this principle: 'There is not a jewel here but it fits, not a beauty but it subserves an end' (*ES* 65). The metaphors Swinburne selects to describe the dense texture and interlacing themes of Rossetti's work are those of weaving and the web, metaphors used by a number of prominent nineteenth-century writers, such as George Eliot in *Middlemarch* (1871–2) and Pater, who had employed them in the 1868 essay that became the 'Conclusion' to *The Renaissance*.[12] In Rossetti's verse, Swinburne asserts, 'No such coarse or cheap stuff is here used as a ground to set off the rich surprises of casual ornament and intermittent embroidery. The woof of each poem is perfect' (*ES* 62–3). Of the conclusion to Rossetti's 'Dante at Verona', he says: 'No words could more fitly wind up the perfect weft of a poem throughout which the golden thread of Dante's own thought . . . gleams now and again at each turn of the warp' (*ES* 74), his poem 'The Stream's Secret' is 'a web of golden fancies and glowing dreams' demanding to be 'unwound and rewoven by the reader's study of it' (*ES* 85), and Rossetti's profound thought is 'a weft of the sun's spinning, a web not of woven darkness but of molten light. But such work as this can neither be unwoven nor recast by any process of analysis' (*ES* 64).

That image of 'molten light' (which also occurred in the Baudelaire essay) alerts us to the fact that throughout this essay and in other of his critical writings Swinburne uses a language of melting and blending, often combined with images of purification and refinement, light or gold, which ultimately derive from alchemical metaphors. Alchemy is a process of refining base substances and unifying opposite elements to make an end product commonly identified as gold, but known variously in esoteric or mystical alchemy as 'The Elixir of Life' or 'The Philosophers' Stone' and believed to confer immortality. Alchemical metaphors were widely used throughout the nineteenth century, especially in the French tradition with which Swinburne was familiar, to illustrate the process by which the literary artist turns his raw materials into a lasting imaginative creation. In describing Rossetti's lasting achievement as a poet, Swinburne characterizes his poetry as 'golden', referring to its 'golden affluence of images' and its 'fleshly sculpture' 'Mailed in gold' (*ES* 65); in his poem 'Dante of Verona', 'All incidents and traditions of the great poet's exile are welded together in fusion of ardent verse to forge a memorial as of carven gold' (*ES* 72). Rossetti's 'The House of Life' is a 'golden house where the life that reigns is love' (*ES* 66), while *Poems* (1870) is 'the gathered flower of youth and ripe firstlings of manhood, a fruit of the topmost branch "more golden than gold"' (*ES* 109). Moreover, like the alchemist, Rossetti is able to unite opposites, as when he brings together sense impressions to create powerful synaesthetic effects: 'Spirit and sense together, eyesight and hearing and thought, are absorbed in splendour of sounds and glory of colours distinguishable only by delight' (*ES* 64). These effects complement the unifications forged by his poetic thought: 'In all the glorious poem built up of all these poems ["The House of Life"] there is no great quality more notable than the sweet and sovereign unity of perfect spirit and sense, of fleshly form and intellectual fire' (*ES* 71). His poem 'Jenny' is another example of amalgamation in that it 'deals with deep and common things; with the present hour, and with all time; with that which is of the instant among us, and that which has a message for the souls of all men' (*ES* 96). And Rossetti himself, uniting qualities such as 'strength, sweetness, affluence, simplicity, depth, light, harmony' (*ES* 103), has

> the rare and ineffable mark of a supreme singing power, an element too subtle for solution in any crucible of analysis, though its presence or absence be patent at a first trial to all who have a sense of taste. All these this poet has, and the mastery over these which melts and fuses into form and use; the cunning to turn his own gifts to service which is the last great apanage of great workmen. (*ES* 104)

Opening his essay by citing Rossetti as a rare example of the 'double-natured genius' (*ES* 60), a successful painter as well as poet, Swinburne returns to the theme in his conclusion: 'here, where both the sister powers serve in the temple of one mind and impel the work of one hand, their manner of service is smooth, harmonious, perfect' (*ES* 105).

Images of transfusion – a word also heavily associated with the processes of alchemy – inform that strand of the essay that concerns itself with translation, a subject of great interest to Swinburne, himself a skilled translator who won the Prince Consort's Prize for Modern Languages at Eton and the Taylorian Scholarship for French and Italian at Oxford. He starts by noticing the poem on Dante already mentioned, calls Rossetti Dante's 'namechild and translator' (*ES* 71), and praises him for the way in which he manages to translate into verse Dante's famous letter that repudiates 'the base conditions of return' from his exile (*ES* 72). He admires the bilingual versions of the song inset in the narrative poem 'A Last Confession', and comments: 'I can hardly say whether the Italian or the English form be the more divine. The miraculous faculty of transfusion which enables the cupbearer to pour this wine of verse from the golden into the silver cup without spilling was never before given to man' (*ES* 76); and he suggests that Rossetti's ability to translate his own English poem into another language replicates his proficiency as both painter and poet (*ES* 77). Later he remarks on Rossetti's sonnet on the pastoral painting then attributed to Giorgione that it 'actually attains to the transfusion of a spirit that seemed incommunicable from one master's hand to another's' (*ES* 90), and, considering Rossetti's verbal–visual parallel works, singles out what he takes to be the most successful 'of the sonnets on the writer's own pictures and designs' (*ES* 90). He subsequently admires Rossetti's translations from French and Italian poetry (*ES* 91), and, selecting as pre-eminent the translation of Dante's passage on Francesca, once more returns to the image of transfusion: 'But here the divine verse seems actually to fall of itself into a new mould, the exact shape and size of the first – to be poured from one cup into another without spilling one drop of nectar' (*ES* 92) Rossetti's 'power of transfusion' as a translator is so great that he can muster a creditable translation of two fragments by Sappho, even though she is, Swinburne believes, properly untranslatable: 'Here is a delicious and living music but here is not – what can nowhere be – the echo of that unimaginable song . . . as of honey dropping from heaven' (*ES* 92). In these figures the substance of poetry, the 'wine of verse' or 'nectar' that Rossetti manages to translate so successfully, is, one suspects, something akin to the immortalizing 'Elixir of Life'.

The theme of immortality that accompanies alchemical imagery is also present in Swinburne's keenness to stress the enduring nature of Rossetti's achievements. Rossetti's 'Jenny' is 'worthy to fill its place for ever as one of the most perfect or memorable poems of an age or generation' (*ES* 96); 'Troy Town' and 'Eden Bower' are 'good certainly, but they are also great: great as no other man's work of the same age and country' (*ES* 97–8). The concluding pages of Swinburne's essay debate the issue of greatness: the fact that any particular age can rarely recognize its own great men, that each age perennially complains of decadence and the lack of greatness. Having summarized Rossetti's credentials for greatness and set him alongside other candidates such as Tennyson, Browning, Barrett Browning, Arnold and Morris, Swinburne in the last lines of his essay sees Rossetti's achievement as perdurable:

> all may see that although, in the perfect phrase of his own sonnet, the last birth of life be death, as her three first-born were love and art and song, yet two of these which she has borne to him, art namely and song, cannot now be made subject to that last; that life and love with it may pass away, but surely no death that ever may be born shall have power upon these for ever. (*ES* 109)

A sub-theme associated with Rossetti's work is that of mystery, as if the poet were indeed an alchemical mystic familiar with esoteric secrets. Rossetti's major work, 'The House of Life', is so complexly organized 'that no guest can declare on a first entrance the secret of its scheme' (*ES* 64). The pervading atmosphere of mystery is partly conveyed through images of depth, as when we are told that Rossetti's thought 'is too sound and pure to be otherwise dark than a deep well-spring at noon may be even where the sun is strongest and the water brightest' (*ES* 64). Elsewhere individual poems are marked with a distinctive quality that sets them apart from the everyday: 'The Card-Dealer' has 'tragic colour and mystic movement' (*ES* 88); 'World's Worth', an early art-catholic poem about a priest, Father Hilary, which Swinburne thought unwisely omitted from *Poems*, details 'the mystery of sense and ardour of soul' (*ES* 89); the sonnet on Giorgione, like the canvas it describes, is 'glad and sad and sacred, unsearchable and natural and strange' (*ES* 90); 'Eden Bower' has 'the mysterious charm as of soundless music that hangs about a serpent as it stirs or springs' (*ES* 98), while some of the later poems that partner Rossetti's paintings of *femmes fatales* show 'the perfect power of mastery over the truth and depth of nature ... the mysteries and majesties of very life' (*ES* 100). Swinburne also reproduces impressionistically the dense, occult and somewhat claustrophobic feel of Rossetti's poetic world where his readers are those 'who would follow the radiant track of this verse through brakes of flowers and solitudes of sunlight, past fountains hidden under green bloom of leaves, beneath roof-work of moving boughs where song and silence are one music' (*ES* 66).

Examination of the figurative language of Swinburne's essay is thus extremely rewarding, for it shows that, far from being merely decorative, it is an elaborate, harmonious and concentrated form of thinking about the chief characteristics of Rossetti's work. While Swinburne's essay may seem too diffuse and lengthy for modern tastes, it is noticeable that Walter Pater's much more succinct essay 'Dante Gabriel Rossetti' (1883) nonetheless borrows heavily from its precursor, reproducing its concerns such as translation, mystery and synthesis, while making subliminal use of its alchemic imagery in expressions like 'To him in the vehement and impassioned heat of his conceptions, the material and the spiritual are fused and blent'.[13] Pater also treats other Swinburneian themes that I have not had time to touch on here, such as the centrality of Love to Rossetti's work and his Catholic Christian aesthetic, which stresses sensuous form as part of its spiritual message. One might note too that, developing Swinburne's theme of mystery, Pater particularly stresses the 'strangeness' of Rossetti's poetry, which in this context can hardly have a homosexual implication – Rossetti is very much the celebrant of heterosexual love – but rather denotes the haunting, claustrophobic, quasi-supernatural world he creates in his verse.

In his earlier essay 'Notes on the Designs of the Old Masters at Florence' (1868), an essay that is a bridge between

Swinburne's 1862 review of Baudelaire and Pater's 1869 essay
on Leonardo, Swinburne had further explored 'the sorrow and
strangeness of things' (*ES* 318). Proposing male androgyny and
latent homoeroticism as key elements in this essay, Thaïs
Morgan has suggested that 'Swinburne's most intense pleasure
as an aesthetic critic is located not in conventional topics such
as the Madonna and the Holy Family, but in portraits of boys
and young men'.[14] This is a surprising claim in that this essay
is most famous for the already mentioned description of
Michelangelo's snake woman, a figure Swinburne describes
with evident relish in an elaborate set-piece generally thought
to be the major influence on Pater's famous passage on
Leonardo's *Mona Lisa*. Certainly Swinburne does describe a
number of images of beautiful boys and youths and a few
instances of androgynous beauty, but it is not clear that these
images have any priority over those of women, which seem
rather more prominent. The women tend to be portrayed as
cool and self-contained while the youths are more animated,
but all the images, irrespective of their sex, are touched by
gravity, sadness or mystery, as in the description of Leonardo's
'Fair strange faces of women full of dim doubt and scorn',
which attest to 'that indefinable grace and grave mystery
which belong to his wildest and slightest work' (*ES* 316), the
designs by Giorgione of both sexes, which bear witness to his
'adorable genius ... "most glad and sad" ' (*ES* 348), and
Michelangelo's work, which 'in its fullness of its might and
beauty has most often a mournful meaning, some grave and
subtle sorrow latent under all its life' (*ES* 318). Morgan tends
to sideline this powerful emphasis on pain, sorrow and
suffering – a kind of metaphysical or philosophical sadomaso-
chism – which Swinburne sees as central to the appeal of this
art. She is also guilty of some adjustment when she says of
Swinburne that 'the most "exquisite" works of the Uffizi, he
declares, are those in which "beauty ... lifts male and female
together on an equal level of loveliness" '.[15] Swinburne in fact
makes no such grand claim for the supremacy of androgynous
art in the Uffizi, merely noting among Giorgione's designs 'a
youth of that exquisite Venetian beauty which in all these
painters lifts male and female together on an equal level of
loveliness' (*ES* 346). Androgyny and male beauty as topics

hardly figure in the essay contemporary with 'Designs', 'Some Pictures of 1868', which concentrates almost exclusively on images of women by modern painters such as Watts, Albert Moore, Leighton, Sandys and Rossetti. They do, however, come back into focus in an essay of 1871, 'Simeon Solomon: Notes on his "Vision of Love" '.

'SIMEON SOLOMON: NOTES ON HIS "VISION OF LOVE" AND OTHER STUDIES' (1871)

Sometime in 1862 or 1863 Swinburne got to know Simeon Solomon (1840–1905), a Jewish homosexual painter whose paintings of mainly classical and Hebraic subjects have recently been enjoying something of a revival.[16] His classical subjects in particular are notable for their androgynous features and hint at sexual ambiguity. There has been a certain amount of speculation as to whether Swinburne and Solomon had a homosexual relationship, although there is no evidence that this was the case. One of Solomon's letters reveals obliquely that Swinburne had asked him if he had ever committed sodomy (a question he would hardly have asked if he and Solomon had performed such an act together), to which Solomon rather nervously (and probably untruthfully) replied in the negative.[17] While this by no means rules out the possibility that a homosexual attraction could have been expressed in other ways, Lionel Lambourne suggests, on the basis of remarks derived from Solomon himself, that he did not find what he was looking for: the friendship was, 'while both flattering and inspirational, not fulfilling. To illustrate Swinburne's flagellation fantasies . . . did not give the consolations of the ideal Uranian relationship which Simeon sought.'[18] Swinburne's interest in unorthodox sexual behaviour meant that he enjoyed participating with like-minded male friends in knowing conversation, jokes and gossip about sexual practices such as lesbianism, homosexuality and flagellation, or what he elsewhere glossed as a 'Rabelaisian exchange of burlesque correspondence between friends who understand the fun' (Feb. 1873; *Letters*, ii. 227). While he frequented a heterosexual flagellant brothel for a time in 1868, it would seem that his interest in sexuality was largely speculative, contributing to a fantasy discourse between men that gave its participants the frisson of illicit excitement. In 1883 Edmond de Goncourt recorded that Oscar Wilde had told him that Swinburne was 'a braggart in the matter of vice, who had done everything he could to convince his fellow citizens of his homosexuality and bestiality, without being in the slightest degree a homosexual and a bestializer'.[19] Early on in his career Swinburne liked to give the appearance of dabbling in 'vice', whereas in fact a good deal of his pleasure was derived from discussing it. A self-parodic poem, 'Poeta Loquitur', published only after his death, announces that

> Some sinners delighting in curses,
>   Though sinful, have splendidly sinned:
> But my would-be maleficent verses
>   Are nothing but wind.[20]

Solomon's letters to Swinburne – Swinburne's side of the correspondence is missing – while containing obvious homosexual references, suggest that he was aware that the poet's real interest was in flagellation and he evidently goes to some effort to provide material that he knows will please his friend. While Swinburne entertained liberal attitudes towards his homosexual friends at this time, he may have blinded himself to the actual (as opposed to the fantasized) expression of their desires, and he seems personally to have been highly ambivalent about the idea of sodomy. Arthur Munby recalls two instances where the topic of homosexuality came up when Swinburne discoursed on Shakespeare's sonnets: on 2 December 1867 he drunkenly upheld 'that hateful theory of their meaning ... talking of them with an air of high moral indignation', while on 2 May 1870 'he expressed a horror of sodomy, yet *would* go on talking about it; and an actual admiration of Lesbianism, being unable, as he confessed, to see that that is equally loathsome'.[21] When Solomon was arrested for 'buggery' in a public place on 11 February 1873 and thereupon ignominiously dropped by his circle, Swinburne wrote to George Powell (another close friend who was possibly homosexual): 'I suppose there is no doubt that the poor little fellow has really been out of his mind and *done* things amenable to law such as done by a sane man would make it impossible for one to keep up his acquaintance and not be cut by the rest of the world as an accomplice?' (6 June 1873; *Letters*, ii. 253).[22] Evidently some kinds of 'sin' were permissible only if they did not assume too fleshly a form.

It is the vague atmosphere of indeterminate desire that colours Swinburne's review of Solomon's illustrated prose poem 'A Vision of Love' and his artwork in general. In 'Simeon Solomon: Notes on his "Vision of Love" and Other Studies', which appeared in the Oxford magazine *The Dark Blue* for July 1871, Swinburne accentuates the ambiguous sexuality of Solomon's subjects, noting how many of his figures are androgynous: 'Many of these, as the figure bearing the eucharist of love, have a supersexual beauty, in which the lineaments of woman and of man seem blended as the lines of sky and landscape melt in burning mist of heat and light' (SS 453).[23] As Thaïs Morgan indicates in an essay on Swinburne and Solomon, Swinburne singles out for praise paintings of Sappho and Antinous, classical subjects that signal lesbian and homosexual desire, as well as images of the pleasure-loving Bacchus and the Roman Heliogalabus (whose debaucheries included sexual acts with men) that glorify ambiguous kinds of masculine beauty.[24] These references are arguably more explicit in their connotation of same-sex desire than in previous essays by Swinburne, and yet, while Swinburne undoubtedly encourages this connotation, again I think it would be wrong to assume that this is the sole or major meaning of the 'perversity' he admiringly locates in Solomon's work. This same-sex resonance is only part of a much wider treatment of a subliminal sexual strangeness that Swinburne celebrates in Solomon and that once more seems more properly identified with sadomasochism. The epicene youths that Swinburne sees in Solomon's designs are notable just as much for their algolagnia as for their suggestive effeminacy. When he says 'There is a mixture of utmost delicacy with a fine cruelty in some of these faces of fair feminine youth which recalls the explanation of a philosopher of the material school' (SS 456), the nameless 'philosopher' – whom he thereafter cites in French – is the Marquis de Sade, a reference passed over by Morgan, who omits the second part of this sentence. Solomon was concerned, as he expressed it to Swinburne (Oct. 1871; *Letters*, ii. 159), that the review would do him harm, but this was probably as much on grounds of the imputed sadomasochism as the homosexuality – de Sade's identity, if correctly deciphered, being unlikely to confer any favours upon him. As in previous essays, however, sadomasochism is not just a matter of sexual pain and pleasure, but part of a metaphysical expression of the ambivalent joy and sorrow of Life itself, which finds its strongest expression in the complexities of sexual and amatory feeling.

Swinburne starts his essay on Solomon by discussing how beauty takes many forms, but stipulating that those who are artists in more than one field, such as a writer and painter like Solomon (or, we might add, Rossetti), are likely to be attracted by 'the mystery in all beauty' (SS 443). It is this 'mystery in all beauty', a development of the 'strangeness' in the Baudelaire essay, the 'mystery' of the Rossetti essay and Pater's 'curiosity and the desire of beauty' in his Leonardo essay of 1869, that is the dominant theme in this essay, and that for Swinburne is made potent by an underlying sense of 'the mystery of the cruelty of things' ('Anactoria', l. 154, Haynes, 51). Like the many-talented Rossetti, Solomon is seen as a unifying figure, and in this case one who can bring together diverse cultural influences: his genius 'holds at once of east and west, of Greek and Hebrew' (SS 444). Praising his combination of these ancient artistic influences in his work, Swinburne notes how Solomon introduces something new into his depiction of beauty. His figures 'have tasted a new savour in the wine of life, one strange and alien to the vintage of old . . . There is a questioning wonder in their faces, a fine joy and a faint sorrow, a trouble as of water stirred, a delight as of thirst appeased' (SS 445). The insistence that Solomon complicates the simplicity of the ancient ideals – his treatment of classic subjects is 'Modern rather than classical . . . in sentiment and significance' (SS 450) – is probably strategic, for Swinburne, like Pater at the conclusion of his essay on Winckelmann, certainly did not endorse 'the bright and serene images of the Classics that had been rendered canonical by Winckelmann's and, in Britain, by Matthew Arnold's studies'.[25]

In his subsequent analysis of Solomon's prose poem 'A Vision of Sleep', Swinburne approves its beauty but feels that as an allegory it is too opaque; unlike other of Solomon's works, it has no internal unity: 'We miss the thread of union between the visions of love' (SS 448). Swinburne's real preference, he makes clear, is for Solomon's designs, and a key element of his interest in these designs is surely indicated by his opening description of 'the admirable picture of Roman ladies at a show of gladiators' (SS 449) – *Habet!* (1865) – a painting that portrays overt voyeuristic sadism. More subtle and complex treatments of pain are found in Solomon's classical studies, which add Hebraic 'violence of feeling or faith' to Greek 'sublime reserve and balance of passion', resulting in 'the sadness which is latent in gladness; the pleasure that is palpable in pain' (SS 450). While Solomon's pictures that convey same-sex attraction, 'the *Sappho* and the *Antinous*', 'bear alike the stamp of sorrow; of perplexities unsolved and desires unsatisfied' (SS 451), this stamp of thwarted troubled love is generic to the majority of Solomon's other designs, such as *Damon and Aglae*, in which a girl is struck with foreknowledge of the end of her affair with her male lover. Swinburne explains he wrote the poem 'Erotion' as a comment on this painting 'to express the subtle passionate sense of mortality in love itself' (SS 453). Detailing other of Solomon's designs that feature groups of youths and girls, a marriage scene, a mass and a group of children gathered around the figure of Love, Swinburne observes: 'In almost all of these there is perceptible the same profound suggestion of unity between opposites, the same recognition of the identity of contraries' (SS 455). That unity of opposites is primarily to be found in the poignant mixed emotional charge of these paintings in which joy and wonder are shadowed by intimations of doubt and pain. Pondering this ambivalence, Swinburne notes that it is often hard to determine 'Whether suffering or enjoyment be the master expression of a face, and whether that enjoyment or suffering be merely or mainly spiritual or sensual . . . hard often to make sure whether the look of the loveliest features be the look of a cruel or a pitiful soul' (SS 455–6), and, linking Solomon with the topic of subject of his early review, he declares 'such studies of complex or it may be perverse nature would have drawn forth praise and sympathy from Baudelaire, most loving of all students of

101

strange beauty and abnormal refinement, of painful pleasures of soul and inverted raptures of sense' (SS 456). One can see why Solomon might well have felt uncomfortable to have his work linked not only to the nameless de Sade but also to Baudelaire, whose poems were still largely known in England only by their scandalous repute, and who is here openly characterized by Swinburne as a connoisseur of sadomasochistic pleasures. Nonetheless, while Swinburne may have overemphasized for his own purposes the sadomasochistic element in Solomon's work, it is undeniably present in the haunted pained look of many of his subjects and is sometimes visible in the activities he represents – the women at the gladiatorial spectacle, for example – or his flagellatory drawings, which he kept for private circulation.

The essay on Solomon is Swinburne's strongest and most pointed critical prose exposition of 'the sadness which is latent in gladness; the pleasure that is palpable in pain' to find publication, and it would be his last. As Morgan has explained, after Solomon's arrest in 1873, the fear of being regarded similarly made Swinburne and others in his circle drop the association and Swinburne's anti-homosexual sentiments become more pronounced after this date. He never reprinted the essay on Solomon – Morgan points out that he omits it from a letter to Theodore Watts (10 May 1873; *Letters*, ii. 242) detailing his prose publications after 1867 – but, perhaps more surprisingly, nor did he reprint his early essay on Baudelaire. This may have been because he regarded this essay as a relatively youthful piece of writing, but it may also have been because, alarmed by Solomon's disgrace, he had decided to play down associations generally perceived as decadent and licentious. In later life Swinburne would insist that he really had had very little in common with Baudelaire (6 Oct. 1901; *Letters*, vi. 153). The interest in 'sensitive cruelty' (SS 456) and 'the great and terrible mystery of beauty' (SS 455) in his critical prose would be considerably muted, a pattern that would be repeated in his poetry, and thereafter was exercised only intermittently in a more robust vein in his personal correspondence.

Arguably, after the Solomon essay, Swinburne loses his early aesthetic or impressionistic style and begins to adopt a more prosaic yet also a more rhetorically elaborate style replete with

Johnsonian mannerisms that, in the last stages of his career, can sound decidedly orotund. If Swinburne's tantalizingly nuanced aesthetic style had come to seem intimately caught up with and germane to the sexual and other complexities he described, did he decide to abandon it on the grounds that it had begun to sound too dangerously suspect as effeminate or decadent? Did he consciously or otherwise try to distance himself from this early style by developing a more masculine literary demeanour more suitable for a sober man of letters? We know that in February 1873, the month of Solomon's arrest, Swinburne was already anxious about the fact that his disreputable publisher John Camden Hotten had 'some papers relating to me in the mass of his collection, of which an unscrupulous man might possibly make some annoying use' (*Letters*, ii. 227). Perhaps *Studies of the History of the Renaissance*, published on 1 March 1873, allowed him to resign his early style to Pater, who could now take up the mantle of the aesthetic critic, and who, after all, had his specific concerns and was evidently primed to pursue them through his own exploration of 'curiosity and the desire of beauty' and 'beauty and strangeness'. Swinburne was always guarded about his influence on Pater, although one notes a shift from his letter of 28 November 1869 to D. G. Rossetti (*Letters*, ii. 58) in which he admits 'I confess I did fancy a little spice of my style, as you say', to his more defensive letter to John Morley of 11 April 1873, in which he cites Pater's declaration of indebtedness and adds 'of course no one else would dream of attributing the merit to a study of my style of writing on such matters', suggesting, unconvincingly, of Arnold, 'I should have said that there was more of *his* style than of mine in Pater's' (*Letters*, ii. 241). Clearly, as Swinburne's editor Cecil Y. Lang comments on the earlier letter, 'Pater, as an esthetic critic, owed more than his prose style to Swinburne and more of his style than is allowed here' (*Letters*, ii. 58, n. 5). In 1873 Swinburne might well have had his own reasons for relinquishing aestheticism to Pater and dissociating himself from any influence on him, another possible subliminal factor being, as he remarked to Powell, that Pater 'is a great friend of poor Simeon's' (*Letters*, ii. 253). *The Renaissance* itself, as Swinburne must have noted, would quickly gain Pater a reputation, in Oxford at least, for encouraging neo-paganism, hedonism and moral negligence. Later Swinburne would claim his acquaintance with Pater 'was of the slightest; I should doubt if we ever met more than three or four times' (7 Mar. 1906; *Letters*, vi. 199).

Whatever the rights of this, Pater nonetheless continued to draw fruitfully on Swinburne's work, and indeed 'Simeon Solomon: Notes on his "Vision of Love"' contains the germ of much that will surface in the important essay 'The School of Giorgione' (1877), included in the third (1888) and subsequent editions of *The Renaissance*. Pater's famous description of the interrelatedness of the arts, which he characterizes with the German term *Anders-streben* – that is, the striving of one art form to blend into or connect with another – evidently owes a great deal to the syntheses of Swinburne's essay and his sense of those 'in whose eyes the boundary lines of the several conterminous arts appear less as lines of mere distinction than of lines of mutual alliance' (SS 443). Moreover, Pater's allied claim that 'All art constantly aspires towards the condition of music' – music being the perfect unity of form and content – is anticipated in the many musical analogies used to describe Solomon's work.[26] Swinburne praises his 'perfect music of outline' and the Keatsian ' "unheard melodies" ' that 'vibrate in the forms of this artist's handiwork' (SS 444). Solomon's written style is 'melodious' and throughout his prose allegory 'there is as it were a suffusion of music, transpiration of light and sound' (SS 446). When Swinburne complains about the opacity and lack of coherence in the allegory, he declares that 'even in cloud there is some law of form, some continuous harmony of line and mass, that only dissolves and changes as "a tune into a tune" ' (SS 447). Turning once more to the designs, Swinburne praises the 'melodious beauty' of Solomon's melancholy subjects, and later notes that 'there is an entire class of Mr. Solomon's designs in which the living principle and moving spirit is music made visible'. While many of these designs figure music-making, in others lacking this theme 'the same fine inevitable sense of song makes melodies of vocal colour and symphonies of painted cadence' (SS 454).

If Swinburne helped Pater fashion a nuanced style that spoke obliquely of sexual complexity, ambivalent emotion and heightened consciousness, he also gave him the foundations for more of his aesthetic philosophy and subject matter than is generally realized. The fact that some of Swinburne's essays, such as the piece on Solomon, are inaccessible and indeed that virtually all Swinburne's prose is out of print (even anthologies of extracts such as Eric Warner and Graham Hough's *Strangeness and Beauty* (1983)) means not only that relations between the two writers are obscured, but that it is hard for a reader without access to an academic library to form any real impression of Swinburne's critical writing. This situation will be partly eased by the publication of Jerome McGann and Charles Sligh's *Swinburne: The Major Poems and Selected Prose* in late 2004, although again the chosen essays appear only in extract form. Though the aesthetic prose style Swinburne pioneered proved pervasive and enduring, it is a sorry irony that so few examples of his own work in that style are currently available to readers today.

Coda: *Tristram of Lyonesse*

The concluding pages of Chapter 2 examined two poems from *Poems and Ballads 2* in which Swinburne, exploring memory through the recurring sights of nature, sounded a predominantly elegiac note. But *Tristram of Lyonesse*, Swinburne's Arthurian epic masterpiece, published in 1882, dispels any notion that plaintive melody is the keynote of his subsequent poetry. More appropriate would be a description taken from his own 'On the Cliffs' (1880): 'No swan-song . . . This is [his] song of life' (*PS* iii. 321). Although Swinburne does not shy away from the pain and tragedy inherent in this tale of fateful love, his ultimate vision is of the lovers at peace and united, and throughout he emphasizes how the fruition and maturation of their love is the perfect expression of natural harmony. The final image of Tristram and Iseult asleep under the sea is meant to solace us with the knowledge that 'We, from the fetters of the light unbound, / Healed of our wound of living, shall sleep sound' (*PS* iv. 11).[1] The composition of the poem, which took place over a period of thirteen years from 1869 to 1882, with an intense burst of creative activity occurring in 1881, can be seen as Swinburne's attempt to search and heal his own wound of living. The poem is in many ways the mature expression of his imaginative thought as well as a pattern for the nature poetry of the later years.

Swinburne had long been interested in the legend of the fateful lovers, having read and enjoyed Matthew Arnold's 'Tristram and Iseult' while he was at Eton ('Matthew Arnold's New Poems', *SAC* 55). His first published poem was 'Queen Yseult', published in an undergraduate magazine in 1857 and heavily influenced by the Arthurian poetry of William Morris (whom he had met while at Oxford). In 1868 Swinburne had apparently begun a poem on Tristram and Iseult but lost the manuscript, which he accidentally left in a cab. The following year he started to think about another attempt and, feeling that Arnold and Tennyson (in *Idylls of the King*) had not been faithful to legend, expressed a wish to Burne-Jones 'to adhere strongly to Fact and Reality – to shun Fiction as perilously close to lying, and make this piece of sung or spoken History a genuine bit of earnest work in these dim times' (*Letters*, ii. 51). His principal sources were the Middle English metrical romance *Sir Tristrem,* as edited by Sir Walter Scott, and Malory's *Morte D'Arthur*. He also indicated his desire to consult François Michel's *Tristram*, an edited collection of medieval metrical fragments, and he would have read the other translations and summaries of the legend included in Scott's edition. He also knew something of Wagner's *Tristan*, and may possibly have read the text of the opera. In writing to Burne-Jones he noted that 'the thought . . . of Wagner's music ought to abash but does stimulate me' (*Letters*, ii. 51). Whether he had actually heard any part of Wagner's *Tristan* at this date is another matter, although he had done so by June 1872, when he wrote a poem on the 'effect' of the overture (*Letters*, ii. 183). *Tristan* did not receive its first full performance in Britain until 20 June 1882, a month before Swinburne published his poem, yet similarities have been noted between the two works, suggesting that Swinburne may have been influenced by Wagner's libretto or the account of the opera given by Auguste de Gasperini in his study *Richard Wagner* (Paris, 1866), which he read in October 1869.[2]

Whether or not this is true, the intricately scored arrangement of Swinburne's composition, with its artful internal echoes and variations, its lyrical finesse and swelling symphonic grandeur, irresistibly suggests musical analogies. Critics have long noted how major passages are linked, such as the majestic invocations of Love and Fate, which open the Prelude and Canto 9 respectively and which, in virtuoso fashion, use the same forty-four rhymes (barring a significant alteration in lines 39–40). Swinburne repeats this achievement in a more modest way in the contrasting petitions to Love that occupy the first ten lines of Cantos 6 and 8, and throughout the poem certain phrasings deliberately evoke others, as, for example, when Swinburne crucially twice draws our attention to major events about to befall Tristram and Iseult ('The last time . . .' (see *PS* iv. 36 and 113)), when he describes their first and last kiss ('And their four lips' (see *PS* iv. 38 and 148)), or when he indicates by her tone of voice the changed nature of Iseult of the White Hands ('I am here' (see *PS* iv. 74 and 145)). The musical analogies are furthered by the use of *leitmotifs* for the lovers and their developing love: Iseult is often compared to flowers and Tristram to the sun, and both lovers and their love to dawn and light. Moreover, the long emotional soliloquies made by Tristram, Iseult and Iseult of the White Hands invariably suggest arias, particularly Iseult's, which is accompanied by a heavily orchestrated storm that rages outside as she speaks. Music as a theme is itself omnipresent: Tristram, a skilled harpist, sings a number of exquisite lyrics, and nature's melodies – birdsong, sea sounds and such – are constantly celebrated. Yet there is another higher thematic of music in so far as concord, in particular the concord of the natural world, is frequently described throughout the poem by allusion to musical harmony.

Shortly after writing to Burne-Jones, Swinburne started the poem proper in December 1869 (*Letters*, ii. 72–3) in swift response to the recently published second instalment of Tennyson's *Idylls*. He strongly disapproved of the way in which the older poet ignored the importance of fate in the Arthurian legend, a legend that properly hinges on the tragic effects of Arthur's unwitting incest with his half-sister. In omitting this and also in imposing an inappropriate mid-Victorian morality on his medieval subjects, Tennyson diminished the story of the love between Lancelot and Guinevere into mere ignoble adultery. Swinburne also objected to Tennyson's demeaning portrayal of the relationship between Merlin and Vivien (the maiden usually known as Nimuë), a relationship that he would elevate in his own poem.[3] And he later called Tennyson's own treatment of the Tristram legend in 'The Last Tournament', published in 1871, 'degraded and debased' (*Letters*, iv. 260). Tennyson's depiction of Tristram as a somewhat boorish and opportunistic adventurer and Iseult as a querulous ageing adulteress can only have added impetus to Swinburne's decision to give what he saw as 'the loveliest of mediaeval legends' (*Letters*, iv. 260), the archetypal narrative of fateful love, the dignity and status it deserved. Edmund Gosse comments: 'Love in its romantic aspect had a perennial attraction for Swinburne, and the tale of Tristram and Iseult was romantic to extravagance. In all the other great stories of the world love had been an appanage or an ornament; in this, for the first time, and in the quivering Celtic abandonment, it was the essence of the event' (*Life*, 260).

Particulars of the Tristram story vary; Swinburne adheres to its romantic core, concentrating on the all-important love relationship. He opens his version of the story at the point where Tristram, the son of the King of Lyonesse and a brave warrior and skilled harpist, is sent to Ireland to escort the king's daughter, the fair Iseult, to Cornwall, where her bridegroom King Mark awaits. Iseult's mother has had a premonition that the marriage may be endangered and as a precaution secretly entrusts Iseult's handmaid Brangwain with a magic potion to be given to the bridal pair on their wedding night, which will ensure their lifelong love and devotion to each other. Unfortunately during the voyage Iseult unwittingly gives the potion to Tristram and drinks of it herself and the couple fall passionately in love with each other. On arrival in Cornwall, Iseult is married to Mark, and, on the wedding night, Brangwain takes Iseult's place in the marital bed to disguise her mistress's loss of virginity. Thereafter the lovers conduct a clandestine affair, which is interrupted when the knight Palamede, visiting the court, pleases Mark with his harp playing. Entranced by his performance, Mark rashly promises to give Palamede any reward he pleases. Palamede asks for Iseult and Mark feels honour-bound to comply. However, after Palamede rides off with Iseult, Tristram rides after them, defeats Palamede in combat, and the lovers escape to live in the woods for a season. Eventually they are discovered in the forest and Mark is subsequently informed of their infidelity. Tristram faces death but manages to break free. In the course of his wanderings he comes, after a period of some years, to Brittany, where he meets another Iseult, the daughter of the king, known as Iseult of the White Hands, who falls in love with him. Tristram marries her, but, mindful of his love of

Iseult of Cornwall, does not consummate the marriage. When Iseult's brother, Ganhardine, finds out that his sister is still a maid, he remonstrates with Tristram, but is pacified when Tristram explains and takes him secretly to Cornwall to show him his true love. Tristram then escapes with Iseult of Cornwall and the couple find sanctuary first at Camelot and then at Joyous Gard, Lancelot's Castle, where they enjoy a temporary union. However, they are once more parted when King Arthur summons Tristram to take arms against the giant Urgan and demands the return of Iseult to Mark. After his successful defeat of Urgan, Tristram returns to Brittany, where he helps a knight recover his abducted wife. Wounded in the conflict, he is nursed by his own wife, Iseult of the White Hands, who is full of bitterness because of his treatment of her. While on his sickbed, Tristram, knowing that he is mortally ill, instructs Ganhardine, his brother-in-law, to go to Iseult in Cornwall and bring her to him. The success or failure of his mission is to be signalled by the white or black sails of his returning ship. Ganhardine returns with Iseult, but Tristram's wife, full of anger and jealousy, tells him that the approaching ship has black sails, and he dies before his true love disembarks. On seeing her dead lover, Iseult immediately joins him in death. Swinburne ends his version of the story with the burial of the lovers by the magnanimous King Mark, who, having learnt the role of the fateful potion, entombs them in a magnificent chapel, which, with the passage of time, is swallowed up by the sea.

Swinburne's narration assumes that the reader already has some familiarity with the legend and tends to be somewhat elliptical, leaving out some of the connecting episodes, which are then told in the form of flashbacks. He explained in the 'Dedicatory Epistle' (1904) with which he prefaced his collected poems that he wrote the poem 'not in the epic or romantic form of a sustained or continuous narrative, but mainly through a succession of dramatic scenes or pictures with descriptive settings or backgrounds: the scenes being of the simplest construction, duologue or monologue, without so much as the classically permissible intervention of a third or fourth person' (*PS* i, p. xviii).

In 1871 Swinburne published his Prelude to *Tristram of Lyonesse* in an anthology entitled *Pleasure: A Holiday Book of*

Prose and Verse edited by James Hain Friswell. This Prelude is sometimes seen as having only a tangential relationship with the poem as a whole, but does in fact set up key ideas and images important to the work. It opens with a long invocation of Love, along with Fate one of the twin powers that, in Swinburne's poetic conception of the universe, motivate and energize all life and action. It then traces out a new astrological calendar in which illustrious romantic heroines name stars that one by one mark the months of the year: thus Helen is January, Hero February and so on. Iseult, linked with April, 'My birth-month star', is 'My singing sign that makes the song-tree flower' (*PS* iv. 8). When this calendar is complete, the narrator ponders the fate of the dead, wondering if they have an afterlife, and, having acknowledged that all must die, decides some dead lives deserve to be rescued from oblivion. To this end he proposes to revive Tristram and Iseult from their mortal sleep with a symbolic kiss of life. He will give

> Out of my life to make their dead life live
> Some days of mine, and blow my living breath
> Between dead lips forgotten even of death.
>
> (*PS* iv. 12)

By sharing his breath and giving of his life to make them live, the Swinburneian narrator blurs the boundaries between himself and the lovers, showing his unity and utter sympathy with them. Thereafter we are to understand that the passions and feelings they experience are also his own. The act of breathing life into the lovers recalls God in Genesis breathing life into Adam, a parallel that is surely intended, for, like Adam and Eve, Tristram and Iseult are an archetypal couple, made in their author's likeness and referred to in the Prelude as 'my twain' (*PS* iv. 12). However, while the 'fall' of Adam and Eve, which takes place when they make the conscious decision to eat from the forbidden Tree of Knowledge, incurs their creator's blame and censure, in Swinburne's poem, the almost immediate 'fall' of Tristram and Iseult, which occurs when they unwittingly drink the magic potion, is sanctioned by their author because it is integral to the greatest love story of all time. Theirs is a fall into love that, though technically sinful or illicit, nonetheless represents the highest and most perfect kind of human passion.

If the poem can be seen to offer an Old Testament parallel, it also positions itself as a secular gospel in which the couple incarnate or embody their author's ideals of love and his wider sense of the vital energies that reverberate through the universe and animate matter. *Tristram of Lyonesse* is an unorthodox but nonetheless strongly religious poem that strives to express a universal spiritual power that inheres in and cannot be separated from the natural rhythms of physical and material existence. We see this in the invocation of love with which the poem opens:

> Love, that is the first and last of all things made,
> The light that has the living world for shade,
> The spirit that for temporal veil has on
> The souls of all men woven in unison,
> One fiery raiment with all lives inwrought
>
> .   .   .   .   .   .
>
> Love, that is root and fruit of terrene things . . .
>
> (*PS* iv. 5, 6)

Nonetheless it is the lovers, seen as part of the cycle or process of the natural world, who communicate this spiritual power most vividly, and it is frequently expressed through images of music, harmony or song. Iseult in Canto 1, 'The Sailing of the Swallow', muses on the mystery of sexual and romantic love,

> that sweet wonder of the twain made one,
>
> .   .   .   .   .   .
>
> Star with star molten, soul with soul imbued,
> And all the soul's works, all their multitude,
> Made one thought and one vision and one song . . .
>
> (*PS* iv. 33)

Thus when, in Canto 2, 'The Queen's Pleasance', Tristram and Iseult make love in the woods outside Tintagel, it is as if nature brings itself into harmony with their union:

> and all the woodland soul was stirred,
> And depth and height were one great song unheard,
> As though the world caught music and took fire
> From the instant heart alone of their desire.
>
> (*PS* iv. 52)

In Canto 8, 'The Last Pilgrimage', Tristram, preparing for his last great deed of chivalry, takes sustenance from the elemental seascape before him:

> The world's half heavenly face,
> The music of the silence of the place,
> The confluence and refluence of the sea,
> The wind's note ringing over wold and lea,
> Smote once more once through him keen as fire that smote,
> Rang once more through him one reverberate note . . .
>
> (*PS* iv. 129)

This reciprocity with the natural world finds its emblem at the heart of the poem in the image of Merlin wrapt in mystic sleep by his lover, the enchantress Nimuë. Dreaming in Broceliande, he

> Feels ambient change in the air and strengthening sun,
> And knows the soul that was his soul at one
> With the ardent world's, and in the spirit of earth
> His spirit reborn to mightier birth
>
> .   .   .   .   .   .
>
> He hears in spirit a song that none but he
> Hears from the mystic mouth of Nimuë
> Shed like a consecration; and his heart,
> Hearing, is made for love's sake as a part
> Of that far singing, and the life thereof
> Part of that life that feeds the world with love . . .
>
> (*PS* iv. 98–9)

On learning of Merlin's song-lapt sleep, Iseult exclaims to Tristram 'Yea . . . some joy it were to be / Lost in the sun's light and the all-girdling sea' (*PS* iv. 99), thereby anticipating her own fate, when she and Tristram, united in death, lie in peace in the chapel beneath 'The light and sound and darkness of the sea' (*PS* iv. 151).

Throughout the poem the couple are seen as being in sympathy or harmony with nature and the natural universe. Their bodies, emotions and the development of their love are repeatedly described through metaphors and analogies drawn from the natural world, and their emotions are frequently coloured or influenced by their responses to natural phenomena; however, the poem also suggests that the natural world very often sympathizes with or takes its cue from the couple,

113

who, as in the example just cited from 'The Queen's Pleasance', seem able to ignite or trigger or inspire chain reactions of natural energies. The lovers, both of whom are seen to be unusually open and receptive to nature, frequently figure as the dynamic heart or centre of elemental power. Thus, for example, in Canto 1, Iseult hearing from Tristram the tragic story of Arthur and Morgause, has pity on them and asks why those who sin unwittingly should suffer:

> 'What good is it to God that such should die?
> Shall the sun's light grow sunnier in the sky
> Because their light of spirit is clean put out?'
>   And sighing she looked from wave to cloud about,
> And even with that the full-grown feet of day
> Sprang upright on the quivering water-way,
> And his face burned against her meeting face
> Most like a lover's thrilled with the great love's grace
> Whose glance takes fire and gives . . .
>
> (*PS* iv. 25–6)

Iseult's enlightened views actually do appear to make the 'sun's light grow sunnier in the sky' as they seem to spark daybreak and set off a series of ensuing reactions in sea, wind, foam, and the fading moon, till

>   the height
> Throbbed and the centre quivered with delight
> And the depth quailed with the passion as of love,
> Till like the heart of some new-mated dove
> Air, light, and wave seemed full of burning rest,
> With motion as of one God's beating breast . . .
>
> (*PS* iv. 26)

Then Iseult in turn responds to this charged atmosphere of passion, drinking it in:

> And her heart sprang in Iseult, and she drew
> With all her spirit and life the sunrise through,
> And through her lips the keen triumphant air
>
> .   .   .   .   .   .
>
> And through her eyes the whole rejoicing east
>
> .   .   .   .   .   .
>
>   yea, she felt

114

Through her whole soul the sovereign morning melt,
And all the sacred passion of the sun . . .

(*PS* iv. 26–7)

Such a passage, demonstrating the complex reciprocal relationship between Iseult and nature, implicates her as the emotional and generative centre of the scene. Swinburne's eroticized language typically blurs its boundaries, telling us also of her sensual awakening and her growing, half-conscious interest in Tristram, and preparing us for the moment near at hand when she will drink the potion and fall irrevocably in love. Indeed the image of the sun as Iseult's lover already hints at the role Tristram will play, for throughout the poem he is repeatedly compared to the sun, light and the new day, and has already been called 'the morning . . . a light to look on and be loved' (*PS* iv. 16).

The pathetic fallacy is the best known of the descriptive devices that imply that nature is in sympathy with the perceiving subject. As it apparently does away with the distinction between the human and the natural, it would seem reasonable to expect to see extensive use of the fallacy in a poem such as *Tristram of Lyonesse*. Ruskin, we recall, defined the fallacy as the imputation of human character and feeling to natural objects by the perceiving subject when under the influence of strong feeling. While Ruskin sanctions certain manifestations of the fallacy if they seem to him to be caused by genuine emotion, he is nonetheless always troubled by the fact that, even when used 'correctly', the fallacy is at root essentially based on deceit and false appearances, thus perverting the book of nature, which is the expression of the Divine Mind. However, while Ruskin is disturbed by the wholesale metaphorical animation of natural objects, he approves of analogies, similes and comparisons which, by employing words such as 'like', 'as' or 'seems', preserve the boundaries between the object and the emotion or character ascribed to it: 'Thus, when Dante describes the spirits falling from the banks of Acheron "as dead leaves flutter from a bough" [*Inferno*, III. 112], he gives the most perfect image possible of their utter lightness, feebleness, passiveness, and scattering agony of despair, without, however, for an instant losing his own clear

115

perception that *these* are souls, and *those* are leaves; he makes no confusion of one with the other.'[4] Such similes or analogies are commonly used in epic poetry, often in an extended form; indeed they are the predominant form of comparison in *Tristram of Lyonesse*, where they consistently draw parallels or mark similitudes between human beings and natural phenomena. For example, regarding Iseult,

> The very veil of her bright flesh was made
> As of light woven and moonbeam-coloured shade
> More fine than moonbeams; white her eyelids shone
> As snow sun-stricken that endures the sun . . .
>
> (*PS* iv. 14)

While Tristram's

> Song sprang between his lips and hands, and shone
> Singing, and strengthened and sank down thereon
> As a bird settles to the second flight,
> Then from underneath his harping hands with might
> Leapt, and made way and had its fill and died . . .
>
> (*PS* iv. 16)

Throughout Canto 5, 'Iseult at Tintagel', Iseult's sorrowful and passionate monologue on the long-absent Tristram is accompanied by sound effects from the elements outside, which convey the inner tumult of her fears and foreboding:

> And as full field charging was the sea,
> And as the cry of slain men was the wind . . .
>
> (*PS* iv. 81)

> And all her soul was as the breaking sea,
> And all her heart anhungered as the wind . . .
>
> (*PS* iv. 82)

It could be argued that in these kinds of analogy the formal markers of comparison – the 'like', 'as' or 'seems' – thus indicate a slight reserve or propriety on their author's part that stops him from fully merging the human and the natural. However, Swinburne's poetry often has the effect of saying or implying more than it means and what is interesting about his

use of these epic comparisons is that they are often so frequent
and so extended and rich in connotation that the reader most
often overlooks or forgets the formal markers of comparison
and runs the two categories together. Thus, for example, we
have the famous description of Iseult's 'unimaginable eyes':

> As the wave's subtler emerald is pierced through
> With the utmost heaven's inextricable blue,
> And both are woven and molten in one sleight
> Of amorous colour and implicated light
> Under the golden guard and gaze of noon,
> So glowed their awless amorous plenilune,
> Azure and gold and ardent grey, made strange
> With fiery difference and deep interchange
> Inexplicable of glories multiform . . .

(PS iv. 14)

As Antony H. Harrison, one of the best commentators on the
poem, remarks: 'Iseult's proportions in this epic simile become
universal. Like Tristram, she is not merely in harmony with the
natural world, she is indistinguishable from it. She contains
elemental creation and is contained by it.'[5] Such amalgama-
tions also take place when one natural object is compared with
another, as when the narrator in Canto 2 juxtaposes the
butterflies that flit over the lovers' bodies with flowers and
snow in so prolonged and detailed a comparison that the
reader sees a white blur of translucent wings and ethereal
petals:

> Fleet butterflies, each like a dead flower's ghost,
> White, blue, and sere leaf-coloured; but the most
> White as the sparkle of snow-flowers in the sun
> Ere with his breath they lie at noon undone
> Whose kiss devours their tender beauty, and leaves
> But raindrops on the grass and sere thin leaves
> That were engraven with traceries of the snow
> Flowerwise ere any flower of earth's would blow;
> So swift they sprang and sank, so sweet and light . . .

(PS iv. 52–3)

Furthermore, in some of Swinburne's epic comparisons the
natural object offered as analogy can itself become a pathetic
fallacy as in

> her mouth
> Was as a rose athirst that pants for drouth
> Even while it laughs for pleasure of desire . . .

(PS iv. 43–4)

And

> her bright limbs palpitated and shrank
> And rose and fluctuated as flowers in rain
> That bends them and they tremble and rise again
> And heave and straighten and quiver all through with bliss
> And turn afresh their mouths up for a kiss,
> Amorous athirst of that sweet influent love . . .

(PS iv. 51–2)

Moreover, throughout the poem the epic comparisons are supported by an overarching series of major pathetic fallacies in which certain elemental powers such as the seasons, dawn, day, sun, moon, earth, sky, rain, wind, lightning and the sea are personified:

> the imperious mirth
> Of wind and light that moved upon the earth . . .

(PS iv. 26)

> Far and fain
> Somewhiles the soft rush of rejoicing rain
> Solaced the darkness and from steep to steep
> Of heaven they saw the sweet sheet lightning leap
> And laugh its heart out in a thousand smiles . . .

(PS iv. 50)

> And the spring loved him surely, being from birth
> One made out of the better part of earth . . .

(PS iv. 62)

> Up sprang the strength of the dark East, and took
> With its wide wings the waters as they shook,
> And hurled them huddling on aheap, and cast
> The full sea shoreward . . .

(PS iv. 125)

Arguably such personifications invariably reflect the lovers' moods and sensations, but, can they, we wonder, strictly be

118

termed 'pathetic fallacies' or false appearances if the religious ethos of the poem suggests that nature really does have a spiritual force of its own? The pathetic fallacy generally suggests that the perceiver's passion or feeling is projected onto natural objects, but Swinburne's poem repeatedly seems to say that feeling resides both in nature and its beholders and that they are thus co-involved and reinforce each other. Thus Tristram, musing on the natural things around him, asks:

> 'These half-born blossoms, born at once and dead,
> Sere brown as funeral cloths, and purple as pall,
> What if some grief and life be in them all?'

(PS iv. 57)

Although Swinburne's telling of the legend comes with a courtly medieval overlay, the original Celtic character of the myth permeates through in the treatment of human beings attuned to the natural world in which they live. Swinburne's elemental pathetic fallacies perhaps suggest remnants of pagan divinities, but they properly testify to a pantheistic world in which an unbounded open-hearted being such as Tristram finds himself corresponding with the energies he feels about him:

> So seemed all things to love him, and his heart
> In all their joy of life to take such part,
> That with the live earth and the living sea
> He was as one that communed mutually
> With naked heart to heart of friend to friend . . .

(PS iv. 62)

Likewise, the lovers are temporarily reunited at Joyous Gard, where

> Day by day
> The mighty moorlands and the sea-walls grey,
> The brown bright waters of green falls that sing
> One song to rocks and flowers and birds on wing,
> Beheld the joy and glory that they had,
> Passing, and how the whole world made them glad,
> And their great love was mixed with all things great,
> As life being lovely, and yet being strong like fate.

(PS iv. 93–4)

They took the moorland's or the bright sea's boon
With all their hearts into their spirit of sense . . .

(*PS* iv. 95)

Max Nordau's objection to Swinburne's early poem 'The King's Daughter', which we examined in Chapter 1, is, in spite of its evident disapproval, rather a good summary of the way in which Swinburne represents 'the external world' in *Tristram of Lyonesse*.

> He does not let the external world express a mood, but makes it tell a story; he changes its appearance according to the character of the events he is describing. Like an orchestra, it accompanies all events which are somewhere taking place. Here nature is no longer a white wall on which, as in a game of shadows, the varied visions of the soul are thrown; but a living, thinking being, which follows the sinful love-romance with the same tense sympathy as the poet, and which, with its own media, expresses just as much as he does – complacency, delight, or sorrow – at every chapter of the story.[6]

Nordau's characterization of the external world as an accompanying orchestra that is in tune with the different phases of the love-romance is a remarkably apt description of the way in which Swinburne conducts the swelling passages of naturalistic detail that elaborate the developing emotional drama. These passages are rich in images of sound, and light, of tides, currents and bodily sensations, various of which merge or blend into each other. Sympathetic readers of *Tristram of Lyonesse* experience themselves as caught up in a web of sensation or immersed in these waves of sound, light and emotion. But, rather than being simply overwhelmed, they come to centre themselves, albeit only fleetingly, in the space occupied by the lovers, and understand that the poem is attuning them to a highly charged level of perception and excitement. Drawing its readers into the vortices, the panoramic whirl and spin of its descriptions, the poem through its synaesthetic blending of sensory phenomena awakens and sustains that intense and heightened pitch of nervous awareness and receptivity that Swinburne calls 'the spirit of sense' or 'the spirit within the sense'. At the same time as the poem formally educates its readers in its philosophy of love and natural harmony, the actual reading of the poetry, if performed attentively, engenders the kind of sympathetic awareness that would allow such philosophy to take root and flourish.

The symbiosis between the individual and the natural world typifies the best of the poems that follow *Tristram of Lyonesse*. The truly outstanding compositions diminish in number but include 'A Nympholept' (1894) and 'The Lake of Gaube' (1899), extraordinary poems that show that Swinburne in his later life was still capable (as many poets are not) of writing at his best. There are also plenty of other poems worth reading. Ventures into the later verse can be daunting, as one has to clear away a thicket of verse consisting, among other things, of assorted elegies, jingoistic appeals and sentimental poems about children, most of them carefully constructed but lacking genuine imaginative energy. However, in addition to a good number of the roundels from *A Century of Roundels* (1883), a not-exclusive list of later interesting poems, some weightier than others, might include 'A Double Ballad of August', 'Heartsease Country' and 'A Ballad of Appeal' (To Christina G. Rossetti), and some sections of the long title poem from *A Midsummer Holiday* (1884); 'To a Seamew', 'Neap-Tide', 'Pan and Thalassius', 'The Interpreters', and the north-country ballads from *Poems and Ballads 3* (1889); 'Loch Torridon', 'On the South Coast', 'A Swimmer's Dream', 'The Palace of Pan', 'Elegy' (for Richard Burton), the elegiac sonnets for Robert Browning, 'A Reminiscence' and 'To a Cat' from *Astrophel* (1894); *The Tale of Balen* (1896); 'In a Rosary', 'The High Oaks', 'Barking Hall: A Year After', 'A New Year's Eve' and 'An Evening at Vichy' from *A Channel Passage* (1904). Many of the best of these later poems draw on nature, landscape and Swinburne's love affair with swimming and the sea, and show the poetic subject's increasing awareness of natural rhythms and his epiphanic immersion in the elemental energies that power the planet.

The survey of Swinburne made in this book can only hope to be partial, but, in introducing the reader to three of Swinburne's major poetic collections, a selection of his most influential aesthetic prose, and a major epic poem, I hope to have given a sense of the richness and diversity of his work and his achievement as one of the outstanding poets of the nineteenth century.

Appendix

Manuscript Transcription: Pasiphae (British Library, MS Ashley 5097, fos. 37–41)
(Watermarked T&JH 1867)

Pasiphae

Daedalus.
O might of man & marvellous handicraft,
What great work have ye done, serving the soul,
Both here & in all places of all time,
Now chiefliest serving, now this goodly shape
Stands excellent, a cunning carven beast,
Made to my mind out of well-laboured wood,
Fit for a fair queen's body to creep in
And hide & suck the liberal juice of joy
Drinking with mere beast's mouth a god's delight!
For with the strong drink of salt-tasted love   10
Shall her desire be saturated & feed
Till it wax faint & glut the belly & womb
At all obscure & delicate orifices,
And at all pores of permeated flesh
Soak itself to the soul with honey-seed,
Sweet stings & pleasurable warm violences
And shoots of fluid flame through the aching blood
And drench of draughts not drunken at the mouth.
This say I now by queen Pasiphae,
As whom the sharp goad of an amorous will   20
Pricks to the bone, biting her flesh with teeth
Immedicable, a wider-waxing wound.
Nor on her dreamless eyelids does the night
Sit peaceable, nor day with staff of gold
Beat off the violent thoughts that vex her brain.
For when man's heart is hunted of such hounds,

Not with oil rubbed nor any balsam grown
Shall it be salved from seizure of their fangs.
But this I bid gods look to; since on earth
There springs no herb for hurts remediable   30
That can shut up such lips of such a wound.
And now with veiled head & august array,
Queenlike she comes forth to the gold-eyed morn.
Hail thou, the lady of this our land, & be
Happy, so be it God gives thee happiness.

   Pasiphae.
Hail thou too, the most subtle hand of men,
Elect of gods for elegance of craft,
And thankworthy; what hap or hope is ours?

D. O queen, good hope is waxen to good hap,
And of fair blossom fruit is fairer born;   40
Look if I bid thee duly cheer or no.

P. O gods, what birth is this then of thy wit?
D. Nay, with bare hands was this thing procreated.
P. A goodly birth & generative of good.
D. So may my spiritual seed bear fleshly fruit –
P. As of what graft incorporate with what stem?
D. To thy glad body & womb impregnated.
P. Thou shewest no shew perspicuous to my sight.
D. Set thy face here & say what shew of shape –
P. I seem then blind or slant of sight in thine?   50
D. Thine eyes drink down beholding what is wrought.
P. Surely the clean shape of a carven cow –
D. So much thou seest, & this with bodily eyes?
P. Hollowed inside & jointed with fit limbs –
D. So thy tongue fitly now sets fit[1] word to word.
P. And fitted with a fell of heavy hair.
D. Seems this to thee then no small subtlety –
P. But rather a feat of some divine device.
D. To have wrought in wood such likeness of a life?
P. Some god then blew breath in between the lips.   60
D. Know that thou seest no god who seest but me.
P. Man, but the gods then over-gave of gifts –
D. Keep thy tongue wary & choose innocuous words –
P. Giving thee thus much more than many men.
D. Lest thine eyes weep for thy mouth's hardihood.

P. O happiest head, O my life's help & stay,

123

Be prosperous, & have praise of men & me
In all time alway; but this one thing more,
This will I ask thee, & spare not thou to say,
In what way having put this strange shape on,   70
I may fare heifer-wise beneath a bull,
Being clothed with cow & quite dis-womanized.

D. And seasonable in sooth this speech of thine
Seems to me spoken, & not improvident,
Woman; for where good counsel dwells with kings
Under one roof & on one seat enthroned
Wears one crown with them, there the land fares well,
But with kings evil-counselled fares to death.
Thus then in brief shalt thou reap all thy will –

P. Blessed of God be thou who hast made me so.   80
D. Here where this hinge turns inward half the flank –
P. O happy doorway to the widening womb.
D. Creep thou close in, hiding thy furtive foot –
P. By covered ways the warm walled garden through.
D. And fitting to the measure of the make –
P. Ah blessed body & bed too sweet for sleep.
D. Thy fair-limbed length & breadth proportionate –
P. Even to the likeness of a four-foot life.
D. Set mouth to mouth, & flesh to wood & take –
P. A sweet thing taken in as sweet a snare.   90
D. That prey thy soul hunts after without hounds.
P. No spoil for my spear, but a spear for me.
D. And hidden in a thicket of curled hair –
P. Grass leafy-locked of a well-wooded field.
D. Catch thou no fearful fawn nor fugitive –
P. Nor happed[2] with hands or any net staked in –
D. Hard by the foliage-hidden fountain-head –
P. But with glad wrestle & strong long sport o' the spear.
D. That washed in warmer wells than where men drink –
P. Such as the beast that sips of grows to god.   100
D. Thou mayst wax glad & glorious of thy womb.
P. Being wounded with one weapon & made whole.
D. Wounded thou sayest, but woundless is thy thought.
P. My thought says healing while my tongue says hurt.
D. Fare as thou wilt then well in deem & deed.

P. Fare thou too Godward all thy life long well,
Who hast holpen me past hope of help to hope.

D. The rest I know not, but give only God
Grace if there be grace in my hands' work here.

   Nurse.

O crowned head of my child Pasiphae,   110
What god is this that drives thee without sail
Before the wild wind of a wandering will
Thro' salt sea-storms of soul's distemperature,
Helmless, a blind hull without spars or mast,
Given to the shipwrecking swift hounds of the air
A shelterless and misadventurous prey?
For by no sun nor starlight piloted[3]
The black night turns thee forth to the grey dawn,
The grey dawn to the golden-footed day,
And the day dying again drives back to night.   120
Nor respite falls upon thee slumberless
Nor rest lies down beside thee, but thine eyes
Like lamps of unfed fire burn all night long
And at wide watch wear out the unpeaceful hours
From the eastern to the western-walking star:
And tears in flame's stead feed them as with flame
And waste & wash with hot & stormy rain
Thy dream-forsaken eyelids; & all day
Thy tempest-shaken spirit shakes thee through
And thy spent body sickens with thy soul.   130
Nor now is night well over here, but yet
The grey-faced dew makes hoar the pasture-lands,
And the low light labours upon the sea,
Furrowing with edgeless plough the unflowering field;
Nor has thy father's fiery wheel incensed
The chill marmoreal waters, nor has dawn
Made wide his ways before him high in heaven.

Notes

INTRODUCTION

1. Lucy Fountain, 'An Evening with Swinburne', *Galaxy*, 12 (12 Aug. 1871), 231–4; 232–3.
2. Arthur Symons, 'Three Contemporary Poets', *London Quarterly Review*, 65 (1886), 238.
3. Margaret and F. R. Oliphant, *The Victorian Age of English Literature* (London: Percival & Co., 1892), 140; Gosse, *Life*, 277.
4. Oscar Wilde, quoted in *The Idler Magazine: An Illustrated Monthly*, 7 (1895), 403.
5. *Transatlantic Dialogue: Selected Correspondence of Edmund Gosse*, ed. Paul F. Mattheisen and Michael Millgate (Austin, Tex., and London: University of Texas Press, 1965), 276.
6. T. S. Eliot, 'Ezra Pound' (1946), in *Ezra Pound, A Collection of Essays*, ed. Peter Russell (London and New York: Peter Nevill Ltd., 1950), 25; Ezra Pound, *ABC of Reading* (London: George Routledge & Sons Ltd., 1934), 64.
7. Edmund Gosse, *Portraits and Sketches* (London: Heinemann, 1912), 11, 13.
8. T. Earle Welby, *A Study of Swinburne* (London: Faber & Gwyer, 1926), 14.
9. Peter Quennell, *John Ruskin: The Portrait of a Poet* (London: Collins, 1949), 204–5, cited Rooksby, 8.
10. Morley would later regret this review, and in later life became an ally of Swinburne's, publishing many of his works in his liberal journal, the *Fortnightly Review*.
11. T. S. Eliot, 'Swinburne as Poet', in *The Sacred Wood: Essays on Poetry and Criticism* (London and New York: Methuen, 1980), 150.
12. T. S. Eliot, 'Isolated Superiority', *The Dial*, 86/1 (1928), 6.

CHAPTER 1. STYLE AND SYMPATHY IN THE EARLY POETRY

1. Edmund Gosse, *Dictionary of National Biography, Second Supplement*, ed. Sir Sidney Lee (London: Smith & Elder, 1912), iii. 460.
2. *George Meredith: The Critical Heritage*, ed. Ioan Williams (London: Routledge & Kegan Paul, 1971), 95, 98.
3. Marie Corelli, *The Silver Domino; or Side Whispers, Social and Literary* (London: Lamley & Co., 1892), 246.
4. Maud Ellmann, *The Poetics of Impersonality: T. S. Eliot and Ezra Pound* (Brighton: Harvester Press, 1987), 43–4.
5. W. B. Yeats, 'The Symbolism of Poetry', in *Essays and Introductions* (London and Basingstoke: Macmillan, 1961), 159.
6. The phrase 'spirit of sense' occurs twice in Shakespeare's *Troilus and Cressida*. See I. i. 58 and III. iii. 106. Definition taken from *The Riverside Shakespeare*, ed. G. Blakemore Edwards *et al.* (Boston: Houghton Mifflin Co., 1974), 449.
7. See the studies by Rosenberg, McGann and Maxwell listed in the Select Bibliography.
8. Max Nordau, *Degeneration* (Lincoln, Neb., and London: University of Nebraska Press, 1968), 98.
9. George Eliot, Review of Wilhelm Riehl's *The Natural History of German Life, Westminster Review* (July 1856), in *Selected Essays, Poems and Other Writings* (Harmondsworth: Penguin, 1990), 110; *Adam Bede* (Harmondsworth: Penguin, 1980), 224.
10. M. C. D'Arcy, SJ, *The Mind and Heart of Love: Lion and Unicorn* (New York: Faber, 1947), 33–4, quoted in Antony Harrison, *Swinburne's Medievalism: A Study in Victorian Love Poetry* (Baton Rouge, La., and London: Louisiana State University Press, 1988), 27.
11. Theodore Watts, review of *Poems and Ballads 2, Athenaeum*, 6 July 1878, 7.
12. Lawrence Lipking, *Abandoned Women and Poetic Tradition* (Chicago and London: University of Chicago Press, 1988), p. xviii.
13. For a copy of the photograph, see Andrew Wilton and Robert Upstone (eds.), *The Age of Rossetti, Burne-Jones & Watts: Symbolism in Britain 1860–1910* (London: Tate Publishing, 1997), 39. For comprehensive discussion of the painting, see its individual entry under Whistler in Tate online (www.tate.org.uk).
14. Swinburne's MS letter of 2 April 1865 to Whistler (Whistler S265) accompanying the first six stanzas of 'Before the Mirror' (Whistler S266), along with an additional sheet evidently written later and containing the remaining three stanzas, are in the

Special Collections at Glasgow University. The concluding third section also exists in a variant draft titled – in a hand other than Swinburne's – 'The Dreamer' in the British Library (MS Ashley 4438, fos. 11, 11b). T. E. Welby saw this variant manuscript, then in the collection of T. J. Wise, and dated it to 1862 – see T. E. Welby, *The Victorian Romantics 1850–70* (London: Gerald Howe, 1929), 52 – but the British Library catalogue assigns it to 1865.

15. See Angela Leighton, 'Introduction II', in *Victorian Women Poets: An Anthology*, ed. Angela Leighton and Margaret Reynolds (Oxford: Blackwell, 1995), p. xxxvii.

16. The bound autograph manuscript of 'Sapphics', watermarked 1865, is in the Special Collections of the Harry Ransom Center, University of Texas – MS file (Swinburne, AC) Works.

17. See Paul Fussell, *Poetic Meter and Poetic Form*, rev. edn. (New York: Random House, 1979), 136–7; Yopie Prins, *Victorian Sappho* (Princeton, NJ: Princeton University Press, 1999), 146.

18. Robert Buchanan, 'Literary Morality', in *David Gray, and Other Essays Chiefly on Poetry* (London: Sampson Low, Son, & Marston, 1868), 246.

19. For 'Pasiphae', see Appendix, p. 122, where the poem is transcribed from BL, MS Ashley 5097, fos. 37–41. See also the limited press editions of the poem by T. J. Wise and Randolph Hughes listed in the bibliography.

20. Among the classical sources are Apollodorus, Virgil's *Eclogue* 6 and *Aeneid* 6, and Ovid's *Ars amatoria*.

CHAPTER 2. SWINBURNE'S POETRY UP TO 1878

1. Sandra Gilbert, 'From *Patria* to *Matria*: Elizabeth Barrett Browning's Risorgimento', in Angela Leighton (ed.), *Victorian Women Poets: A Critical Reader* (Oxford: Blackwell, 1996), 24–52.

2. The best biographies are Bolton King, *The Life of Mazzini* (Everyman's Library; London: Dent, 1912), and Dennis Mack Smith, *Mazzini* (New Haven, Conn., and London: Yale University Press, 1994).

3. Swinburne remembered Saffi affectionately in the dedication to his drama *Marino Faliero* (1885), and two poems entitled 'In Memory of Aurelio Saffi' (1890, 1897), reprinted in *Astrophel* (1894) and *A Channel Passage* (1904) respectively. Orsini is celebrated in 'For a Portrait of Felice Orsini' in *Studies in Song* (1880) and mentioned in 'A Song of Italy' (1867) as 'the foiled tyrannicide' (*PS* ii. 258).

4. See, e.g., Maura O'Connor, *The Romance of Italy and the English Imagination* (Basingstoke: Macmillan, 1998), and Harry W. Rudman, *Italian Nationalism and English Letters: Figures of the Risorgimento and Victorian Men of Letters* (London: G. Allen & Unwin, 1940).

5. Samuel C. Chew, *Swinburne* (London: John Murray, 1931), 100.

6. These were 'Ode on the Insurrection in Candia' (March 1867), 'The Halt before Rome' (Nov. 1867), 'An Appeal' (Nov. 1867), 'Siena' (June 1868), 'A Watch in the Night' (Dec. 1868) and 'Super Flumina Babylonis (Oct. 1869).

7. *English Songs of Italian Freedom*, ed. George Macaulay Trevelyan (London: Longmans, Green & Co., 1911), 221.

8. Stephanie Kuduk, ' "A Sword of a Song": Swinburne's Republican Aesthetics in *Songs before Sunrise*', *Victorian Studies*, 43/2 (2001), 253–78; 274.

9. Terry Meyers, 'Swinburne, Shelley, and *Songs before Sunrise*', in Rikky Rooksby and Nicholas Shrimpton (eds.), *The Whole Music of Passion: New Essays on Swinburne* (Aldershot: Scolar Press, 1993), 40–51; Alison Milbank, *Dante and the Victorians* (Manchester and New York: Manchester University Press, 1998), 78.

10. See, e.g., A. E. Housman, 'Swinburne', *Cornhill Magazine*, 177 (1969), 386.

11. Gilbert, 'From *Patria* to *Matria*', 27, 28.

12. Alison Chapman, 'Risorgimenti: Spiritualism, Politics and Elizabeth Barrett Browning', in Alison Chapman and Jane Stabler (eds.), *Unfolding the South: Nineteenth-Century British Women Writers and Artists in Italy* (Manchester: Manchester University Press, 2003), 76–7.

13. Edgar Holt, *Giuseppe Mazzini: The Great Conspirator* (London: Dennis Dobson, 1967), 107.

14. Joseph Mazzini, 'The Duties of Man' (1858), in *Life and Writings*, 6 vols. (London: Smith, Elder & Co., 1864–70), iv. 284, 378.

15. *Mazzini's Letters to an English Family 1844–1872*, ed. E. F. Richards, 3 vols. (London: John Lane, 1920–2), iii. *1861–72*, 196.

16. The paintings in San Domenico are 'The Swooning of Saint Catherine' and 'The Ecstasy of Saint Catherine'. The painting of Christ known as 'Christ at the Column', held in the nineteenth century in the nearby Galleria (or Accademia) delle Belle Arti, is now in the Pinacoteca Nazionale di Siena. Swinburne's narrator addresses Sodoma as 'Razzi', an evident misprint for 'Bazzi', perpetuated in editions of *Songs before Sunrise* after 1871.

17. Corelli's disapproval did not prevent her sending Swinburne an unctuous fan letter (British Library, MS Ashley 5752, fos. 31–3),

dated 31 May 1883, enclosing a spray of orange blossom taken from the grave of Keats, and hailing him as 'the only truly great poet now living in England'.

18. See Coulson Kernahan, *Swinburne As I Knew Him* (London and New York: John Lane, The Bodley Head, 1919), 52.

19. Swinburne wrote to Watts in 1874: 'If I write any more necrological elegies on deceased poets, I shall be taken for the undertakers' laureate' (*Letters*, ii. 334).

20. Georges Lafourcade, *Swinburne: A Literary Biography* (London: G. Bell & Sons, 1932), 226.

21. The manuscript of 'North and South' is at the British Library – India Office, in MSS Eur. F. 127/470.

22. In Richard J. Hutchings and Raymond V. Turley, *Young Algernon Swinburne* (Brighstone, Isle of Wight: Hunneyhill Publications, 1978), 29, the authors cite an 1849 description of 'a magnificent Laurustina hedge' in the garden of the house next door to The Orchard.

23. Coulson Kernahan, *In Good Company: Some Personal Recollections* (London and New York: John Lane, Bodley Head, 1927), 26.

24. Ross C. Murfin, *Swinburne, Hardy, Lawrence and the Burden of Belief* (Chicago and London: University of Chicago Press, 1978), 162.

25. Although 'A Forsaken Garden' was published later in 1876, Swinburne made it the immediate predecessor of 'Relics' in *Poems and Ballads 2*, indicating the affinity between the two poems.

26. 'A Vision of Spring in Winter' was published in April 1875 in the *Fortnightly Review*. The British Library draft manuscript (MS Ashley A1896, fos. 68–69b), showing Swinburne's methods of composition, is transcribed with a commentary in Jerome McGann, *Swinburne: An Experiment in Criticism* (Chicago and London: University of Chicago Press, 1972), 227–35.

CHAPTER 3. SWINBURNE'S AESTHETIC PROSE

1. Reissued in its original unexpurgated manuscript form as *A Year's Letters*, ed. F. J. Sypher (New York: New York University Press, 1974; repr. London: Peter Owen, 1976).

2. 'Clarimonde' ('La Morte amoureuse'), in Théophile Gautier, *One of Cleopatra's Nights and Other Fantastic Romances*, tr. Lafcadio Hearn (New York: Worthington Co., 1886), 71. Hearn's translations of Gautier's stories are particularly fine.

3. 'Leonardo da Vinci', in *The Works of Théophile Gautier*, ed. and tr. F. C. de Sumichrast, 20 vols. (London: George Harrap, 1900–3), ix (1901), 277.

4. Quoted in 'The Louvre', in ibid. 43.

5. *Shelley's Poetry and Prose*, ed. Donald H. Reiman and Sharon B. Powers (New York and London: Norton, 1977), 242.

6. Thomas Medwin first published 'Notes' by Shelley in the *Athenaeum* for 1832, and then reprinted them as 'Critical Notices of Sculpture in the Florentine Gallery' in *The Shelley Papers* (London: Whittaker, Treacher, & Co., 1833), 138–51, giving some additional examples in *The Life of Percy Bysshe Shelley*, 2 vols. (London: Thomas Cautley Newby, 1847), i. 352–6. His first selection can also be found in Mary Shelley, *Essays, Letters from Abroad, Translations and Fragments*, 2 vols. (London: Edward Moxon, 1840), ii. 263–74; For a modern text with numerous small variations, see *Shelley's Prose*, ed. David Lee Clark (London: Fourth Estate, 1988), 343–53.

7. Text from *The Shelley Papers*, 142; see also *Shelley's Prose*, 349.

8. Walter Pater, 'Romanticism' (1876), republished as 'Postscript', in *Appreciations, With an Essay on Style* (London: Macmillan & Co., 1889, 1898), 258.

9. Thaïs Morgan, 'Reimagining Masculinity in Victorian Criticism: Swinburne and Pater', *Victorian Studies* 36/3 (1993), 315–32.

10. Swinburne read the 'Hymn' to William Bell Scott in December 1862. 'Dolores' was written in 1865. See *Letters*, i. 125 (May–June 1865).

11. Pater first uses this phrase in his essay on 'Winckelmann' (1867). See Walter Pater, *The Renaissance*, ed. Adam Phillips (World's Classics; Oxford: Oxford University Press, 1986), 144. It recurs in his revised 1878 version of his essay 'The Myth of Demeter and Persephone', reprinted in *Greek Studies* (1895). The phrase 'worship of sorrow' is Carlyle's expression (*Sartor Resartus*, bk. 2, ch. 9) for Goethe's phrases 'das Heiligtum des Schmertzes' and 'die göttliche Tiefe des Leidens' in *Wilhem Meister's Wanderjahre*, bk. 2, ch. 2. My thanks to Stefano Evangelista for this information.

12. Walter Pater, 'Poems by William Morris', published in the *Westminster Review* (1868), repr. in *Pre-Raphaelitism: A Collection of Critical Essays*, ed. James Sambrook (Chicago and London: University of Chicago Press, 1974), 115; *The Renaissance*, 152.

13. Walter Pater, 'Dante Gabriel Rossetti', in *Appreciations*, 221.

14. Morgan, 'Reimagining Masculinity', 326.

15. Ibid. 327.

16. A number of Solomon's paintings, including some of those discussed by Swinburne in his essay, can now be seen online. See the Simeon Solomon Research Archive http://www.fau.edu/Solomon/ and another selection at http://www.artmagick.com/artists/solomon.aspx; accessed 22 Apr. 2004.

17. See Solomon's letter of 10 May 1871 (*Letters*, ii. 142) and the helpful explanatory article by John Y. LeBourgeois, 'Swinburne and Simeon Solomon', in *Notes and Queries*, NS 20 (1973), 91–5. LeBourgeois interprets the letter more specifically than I do, in assuming that Swinburne asked Solomon if he had had homosexual relations with the defendants in the recent Boulton and Park trial referred to in subsequent letters. But the conclusion drawn is still pertinent: 'it seems sufficiently clear that Swinburne was not sure whether Solomon was or was not a homosexual' (p. 93), or, we might rather say, what form his homosexuality took.

18. Lionel Lambourne, 'Simeon Solomon: Artist and Myth', in *Solomon: A Family of Painters* (London: Inner London Educational Authority, 1985), 25–6.

19. Entry for Saturday, 21 Apr. 1883, in *Pages from the Goncourt Journal*, ed. and tr. Robert Baldick (Harmondsworth: Penguin Books, 1984), 284. On the publication of the *Journal*, Wilde hastily denied (letter of 17 Dec. 1891) that he had made any such remarks about Swinburne's personal life, blaming his own imperfect French for Goncourt's misunderstanding.

20. I use the text given in *The Oxford Anthology of English Literature*, ed. Frank Kermode and John Hollander, 2 vols. (New York: Oxford University Press, 1973), ii. *1800–The Present*, 1461.

21. Derek Hudson Munby, *A Man of Two Worlds: The Life and Diaries of Arthur J. Munby* (London: John Murray, 1972), 246, 283. This horror of sodomy/physical homosexuality and admiration for lesbianism was shared by Swinburne's French precursors Gautier and Baudelaire. I see no compelling reason, as some critics have suggested, for regarding these men's writing about lesbianism as a cover for male homosexuality.

22. Solomon and his companion, a 60-year-old stableman called George Roberts, were charged with attempting to commit buggery (that is, 'conspiracy to commit buggery', which during the period 1861–85 carried a maximum charge of two years) and indecent exposure. Roberts was sentenced to eighteen months' hard labour, while Solomon, who had been released on bail on 24 February, got off with a fine and the obligation to 'appear when called upon'. See Gayle Seymour, 'The Trial and its Aftermath', in *Solomon: A Family of Painters*, 28. For a copy of the indictment, see Wendell Stacy Johnson, *Living in Sin: The Victorian Sexual Revolution* (Chicago: Nelson-Hall, 1979), 165–6. Swinburne's question about Solomon's mental state may relate to the probably unfounded rumour that, after his release from jail, Solomon had been detained in an asylum.

23. Some key extracts from the essay on Solomon can be found in *Strangeness and Beauty: An Anthology of Aesthetic Criticism 1840–1910*, ed. Eric Warner and Graham Hough, 2 vols. (Cambridge: Cambridge University Press, 1982), i, 255–8.
24. Thaïs Morgan, 'Perverse Male Bodies: Simeon Solomon and Algernon Charles Swinburne', in Peter Horne and Reina Lewis (eds.), *Outlooks: Lesbian and Gay Sexualities and Visual Cultures* (London: Routledge, 1996), 79.
25. Stefano Evangelista, ' "Outward Nature and the Moods of Men": Romantic Mythology in Pater's Essays on Dionysus and Demeter', in Laurel Brake *et al.* (eds.), *Walter Pater: Transparencies of Desire* (Greensboro, NC: ELT Press, 2002), 108.
26. Pater, *The Renaissance*, 85, 86.

CODA: *TRISTRAM OF LYONESSE*

1. References to *Tristram* are to volume iv of the 1904 edition of the poems, but other subsequent editions – the Golden Pine (1917), the Heinemann two-volume edition of 1924 – preserve the same pagination.
2. For more information on Swinburne's sources, see the articles by Staines, Byrd Davies, Sypher and Sillars listed in the Select Bibliography.
3. See Swinburne's essay 'Under the Microscope' (1872), in which he deplores Tennyson's treatment of Merlin and Vivien.
4. John Ruskin, 'Of the Pathetic Fallacy', ch. 12 in *Modern Painters 3*, in *The Works of John Ruskin*, ed. E. T. Cook and Alexander Wedderburn, 39 vols. (London and New York: George Allen and Longmans, Green and Co., 1903–12), v (1904), 206.
5. Antony H. Harrison, *Swinburne's Medievalism: A Study in Victorian Love Poetry* (Baton Rouge, La., and London: Louisiana State University Press, 1988), 105.
6. Max Nordau, *Degeneration* (Lincoln, Neb., and London: University of Nebraska Press, 1968), 98.

APPENDIX: 'PASIPHAE'

1. In their transcriptions both Wise and Hughes omit 'fit', but the word remains uncancelled in Swinburne's MS.
2. According to the *OED*, 'happed' is an obsolete verb meaning 'seized'.
3. An alternative uncancelled line is superscribed: 'For both of suns and stars unpiloted'.

Select Bibliography

MANUSCRIPT COLLECTIONS

The largest collection of Swinburne manuscripts is held by the British Library, London. A list of its holdings can be accessed online. Other substantial collections can be found at the Bodleian Library, Oxford, the Brotherton Library, Leeds, and in the Special Collections of the Harry Ransom Research Center, University of Texas, Austin. Other collections include Georgetown University, the Edith S. and John S. Mayfield Collections at Syracuse University, the Symington Collection at Rutgers University, the Huntingdon Library, the Pierpont Morgan Library, the Kerr Collection at the University of Michigan, and Balliol College, Oxford.

WORKS BY SWINBURNE

William Blake: A Critical Essay, 2nd edn. (London: John Camden Hotten, 1868).
Essays and Studies (London: Chatto & Windus, 1875).
Miscellanies (London: Chatto & Windus, 1886).
A Study of Ben Jonson (London: Chatto & Windus, 1889).
Studies in Prose and Poetry (London: Chatto & Windus, 1894).
The Poems of Algernon Charles Swinburne, 6 vols. (London: Chatto & Windus, 1904).
The Tragedies of Algernon Charles Swinburne, 5 vols. (London: Chatto & Windus, 1905).
Lady Maisie's Bairn and Other Poems (London: printed for private circulation, 1915). 20 copies printed. One of T. J. Wise's limited edition pamphlets containing the first publication of 'Pasiphae', pp. 33–41.
Tristram of Lyonesse (Golden Pine Edition; London: William Heinemann Ltd, 1917).

Posthumous Poems by Algernon Charles Swinburne, ed. Edmund Gosse and Thomas J. Wise (London: William Heinemann, 1917).

Swinburne's Collected Poetical Works, 2 vols. (London: William Heinemann Ltd, 1924).

The Complete Works of Algernon Charles Swinburne, ed. Edmund Gosse and Thomas James Wise, 20 vols. (Bonchurch Edition; London and New York: William Heinemann and Gabriel Wells, 1925–7). This, the standard edition of Swinburne's works, is not complete and the texts are unreliable. Although useful to consult, it is preferable to cite the editions published in Swinburne's lifetime.

Swinburne's Hyperion and Other Poems, ed. Georges Lafourcade (London: Faber, 1927).

Pasiphaë: A Poem, ed. Randolph Hughes (London: privately printed at Golden Cockerell Press, 1950). Press edition limited to 500 copies.

Lesbia Brandon, ed. Randolph Hughes (London: Falcon Press, 1952).

The Swinburne Letters, ed. Cecil Y. Lang, 6 vols. (New Haven: Yale University Press, 1959–62). An indispensable resource.

New Writings by Swinburne, ed. Cecil Y. Lang (Syracuse, NY: Syracuse University Press, 1964).

Swinburne Replies: Notes on Poems and Reviews, Under the Microscope, Dedicatory Epistle, ed. C. K. Hyder (Syracuse, NY: Syracuse University Press, 1966).

Swinburne as Critic, ed. C. K. Hyder (London and Boston: Routledge & Kegan Paul, 1972). A well-edited collection of some of Swinburne's key essays, including his review of Baudelaire.

A Year's Letters, ed. Francis Jacques Sypher (New York: New York University Press, 1974; London: Peter Owen, 1976).

Algernon Charles Swinburne: Selected Poems, ed. L. M. Findlay (Manchester: Carcanet Press, Fyfield Books, 1982, repr. 1987, 2002).

'Algernon Charles Swinburne', in *Strangeness and Beauty: An Anthology of Aesthetic Criticism 1840–1910*, ed. Eric Warner and Graham Hough, 2 vols. (Cambridge: Cambridge University Press, 1983), i. 221–58. Contains extracts from some key prose works, including the essay on Solomon.

Algernon Charles Swinburne, introduced by James P. Carley (Arthurian Poets Series; Woodbridge: Boydell Press, 1990). An unannotated selection of Swinburne's Arthurian poems, including *Tristram of Lyonesse*.

The Works of Algernon Charles Swinburne, ed. Robert Laurence Binyon (The Wordsworth Poetry Library; Ware: Wordsworth Editions Ltd., 1995). Reprint of the World's Classics, Oxford University Press edition of 1939.

Algernon Charles Swinburne, ed. Catherine Maxwell (Everyman's Poetry; London: J. M. Dent, 1997).

Poems and Ballads & Atalanta in Calydon, ed. Kenneth Haynes (Harmondsworth: Penguin, 2000). Excellent annotations. Also contains 'Notes on Poems and Reviews'.

Uncollected Letters of Algernon Charles Swinburne, ed. Terry Meyers, 3 vols. (London: Pickering & Chatto, 2004). One of the most important scholarly publications in recent years. Meyers supplements and updates Lang's valuable edition of the *Letters*.

Swinburne: The Major Poems and Selected Prose, ed. Jerome McGann and Charles Sligh (New Haven and London: Yale University Press, 2004.) The best modern anthology of Swinburne's writings.

BIBLIOGRAPHIC RESOURCES

Beetz, Kirk H., *Algernon Charles Swinburne: A Bibliography of Secondary Works 1861–1980* (Metuchen, NJ: Scarecrow Press, 1982). Extremely useful guide to critical work on Swinburne. For more recent criticism, see Louis below.

Burnett, Timothy A. J., *The British Library Catalogue of the Ashley Manuscripts*, 2 vols. (London: British Library, 1999). Provides a complete list of the extensive collection, including Swinburne manuscripts, owned by the notorious Thomas J. Wise, now in the British Library.

Hyder, Clyde K. (ed.) *Swinburne: The Critical Heritage* (London: Routledge & Kegan Paul, 1970). A useful selection of the Victorian critical response to Swinburne's work.

—— *Swinburne's Literary Career and Fame* (Durham, NC: Duke University Press, 1933, repr. New York: AMS Press, 1984).

Louis, Margot K., 'The Year's Work in Victorian Poetry: Swinburne', *Victorian Poetry* annually. An excellent yearly review of the recent work on Swinburne.

Meyers, Terry, 'Algernon Charles Swinburne', in *The Cambridge Bibliography of English Literature*, 3rd edn., iv. *1800–1900*, ed. Joanne Shattock (Cambridge: Cambridge University Press, 1999), columns 817–36.

Wise, Thomas J., *A Bibliography of the Writings in Verse and Prose of Algernon Charles Swinburne*, 2 vols. (London: privately printed, 1919). Wise's habit of passing off as genuine his forged editions of Swinburne's works means readers should proceed with caution, but these volumes contain interesting photographs, facsimiles and source material. This bibliography is reprinted (minus photographs) as volume xx of Gosse and Wise's *The Complete Works of Algernon Charles Swinburne*.

LITERARY BIOGRAPHIES

Chew, Samuel, *Swinburne* (London: John Murray, 1931). Contains a sympathetic chapter on *Songs before Sunrise* and a useful overview of the prose.

Fuller, Jean Overton, *Swinburne: A Critical Biography* (London: Chatto & Windus, 1968).

Gosse, Edmund, *The Life of Algernon Charles Swinburne* (London: Macmillan, 1917). Standard reading, though contains some inaccuracies.

Henderson, Philip, *Swinburne: Portrait of a Poet* (London: Macmillan, 1974).

Hutchings, Richard J., and Turley, Raymond V., *Young Algernon Swinburne* (Brighstone, Isle of Wight: Hunneyhill Publications, 1978).

Lafourcade, Georges, *La Jeunesse de Swinburne*, 2 vols. (Paris and London: Société d'Édition, Les Belles Lettres and Humphrey Milford, Oxford University Press, 1928).

—— *Swinburne: A Literary Biography* (London: G. Bell & Sons, 1932).

Panter-Downes, Mollie, *At the Pines: Swinburne and Watts-Dunton in Putney* (London: Hamish Hamilton, 1971). Engaging study of Swinburne's later years.

Rooksby, Rikky, *A. C. Swinburne: A Poet's Life* (Aldershot: Scolar Press, 1997). The best modern biography. Incorporates new research.

Thomas, Donald, *Swinburne: The Poet in his World* (London: Weidenfeld & Nicolson, 1979).

Welby, T. E., *A Study of Swinburne* (London: Methuen & Co., 1926).

CRITICAL MONOGRAPHS

Connolly, T. E., *Swinburne's Theory of Poetry* (New York: New York State University Press, 1964).

Fletcher, Ian, *Swinburne* (Longman Writers and their Work Series, no. 228; Harlow: Longman, 1973).

Harrison, Antony H., *Swinburne's Medievalism: A Study in Victorian Love Poetry* (Baton Rouge, La., and London: Louisiana State University Press, 1988). Particularly strong on *Tristram of Lyonesse*.

Louis, Margot K., *Swinburne and his Gods: The Roots and Growth of an Agnostic Poetry* (Montreal: McGill-Queen's University Press, 1990).

McGann, Jerome, *Swinburne: An Experiment in Criticism* (Chicago and London: Chicago University Press, 1972). Still simply the best critical book on Swinburne.

McSweeney, Kerry, *Tennyson and Swinburne as Romantic Naturalists* (Toronto: University of Toronto Press, 1981).

Peters, Robert, *The Crowns of Apollo: Swinburne's Principles of Literature and Art* (Detroit: Wayne State University Press, 1965). Good study of the critical prose.

Raymond, Meredith B., *Swinburne's Poetics: Theory and Practice* (The Hague and Paris: Mouton, 1971).

Riede, David, *Swinburne: A Study of Romantic Myth-Making* (Charlottesville, Va.: University Press of Virginia, 1978).

Rooksby, Rikky, and Shrimpton, Nicholas (eds.), *The Whole Music of Passion: New Essays on Swinburne* (Aldershot: Scolar Press, 1993). A very useful collection, which contains essays by some noted Swinburne scholars. Rooksby's historical survey of Swinburne criticism is invaluable.

ARTICLES AND BOOK CHAPTERS

Alexander, Jonathan, 'Sex, Violence and Identity: A. C. Swinburne and the Uses of Sadomasochism', *Victorian Newsletter*, 90 (1996), 33–6.

Alkalay-Gut, Karen, 'Aesthetic Perversions and Swinburne's "Les Noyades" ', *Journal of Pre-Raphaelite Studies*, NS 6 (Spring 1997), 53–63.

Bowra, Maurice, 'Atalanta in Calydon', in *The Romantic Imagination* (Oxford: Oxford University Press, 1950; repr. London: Oxford University Press, 1961), 221–44.

Bristow, Joseph (ed.), *The Cambridge Companion to Victorian Poetry* (Cambridge: Cambridge University Press, 2000). Swinburne mentioned in a number of different essays.

Buckler, William E., 'The Poetry of Swinburne: An Essay in Critical Reinforcement', in *The Victorian Imagination: Essays in Aesthetic Exploration* (Brighton: Harvester Press, 1980), 227–59. Thoughtful overview of Swinburne's œuvre.

Bullen, J. B., *The Pre-Raphaelite Body: Fear and Desire in Painting, Poetry and Criticism* (Oxford: Clarendon Press, 1998). Swinburne mentioned frequently.

Byrd Davis, Mary, 'Swinburne's Use of his Sources in *Tristram of Lyonesse*', *Philological Quarterly*, 55 (1976), 96–112.

Dellamora, Richard, 'The Poetic Perversities of A. C. Swinburne', in *Masculine Desire: The Sexual Politics of Victorian Aestheticism* (Chapel Hill, NC, and London: University of North Carolina Press, 1990), 69–85.

Eliot, T. S., 'Swinburne as Poet' (1920), in *The Sacred Wood: Essays on Poetry and Criticism* (London: Methuen, 1980), 144–50. Establishes an influential, arguably limited, view of Swinburne's poetry.

—— 'Swinburne as Critic' (1920), in *The Sacred Wood: Essays on Poetry and Criticism* (London: Methuen, 1980), 17–24.

Freeman, Nicholas, ' "Falling into Philistine Hands": Swinburne's Transgressive Correspondence', in Jennifer Wagner-Lawlor (ed.), *The Victorian Comic Spirit: New Perspectives* (Aldershot: Ashgate, 2000), 173–89.

Fricke, Douglas C., 'Swinburne and the Plastic Arts: *Poems and Ballads I* (1866)', *Pre-Raphaelite Review*, 1 (1977), 57–79.

Guzynski, Elizabeth A., 'Oedipus is Burning: Fate, Desire and Masochism in Algernon Charles Swinburne's *Atalanta in Calydon*', *Nineteenth-Century Literature*, 54/2 (1999), 549–66.

Harrison, Antony H., 'The Aesthetics of Androgyny in Swinburne's Early Poetry', *Tennessee Studies in Literature*, 23 (1978), 87–99.

—— 'The Swinburnean Woman', *Philological Quarterly*, 58 (1979), 90–102.

—— 'Eros and Thanatos in Swinburne's Poetry: An Introduction', *Journal of Pre-Raphaelite Studies*, 2/1 (1981), 22–35.

—— 'Swinburne's Losses: The Poetics of Passion', *English Literary History*, 49 (1982), 689–706.

Kuduk, Stephanie, ' "A Sword of a Song": Swinburne's Republican Aesthetics in *Songs before Sunrise*', *Victorian Studies*, 43/2 (2001), 253–78.

Laity, Cassandra, 'H.D. and A. C. Swinburne: Decadence and Sapphic Modernism', in Karla Jay and Joanne Glasgow (eds.), *Lesbian Texts and Contexts: Radical Revisions* (London: OnlyWomen Press, 1992), 217–40.

—— *H.D. and the Victorian Fin de Siècle* (Cambridge: Cambridge University Press, 1996), 32–42 and *passim*.

Lane, Christopher, 'Love's Vicissitudes in Swinburne's *Lesbia Brandon*', in *The Burdens of Intimacy: Psychoanalysis and Victorian Masculinity* (Chicago and London: University of Chicago Press, 1999), 73–92.

Maxwell, Catherine, ' "Beneath the woman's and the water's kiss": Swinburne's Metamorphoses', in *The Female Sublime from Milton to Swinburne: Bearing Blindness* (Manchester: Manchester University Press, 2001), 178–221.

McGhee, Richard, 'Swinburne and Hopkins', in *Marriage, Duty and Desire in Victorian Poetry and Drama* (Lawrence, Kan.: The Regents Press of Kansas, 1980), 177–232. Thoughtful assessment of some less-well-known works including *Erectheus*.

Milbank, Alison, 'Swinburne and Mazzini: The Ideal in the Real', in *Dante and the Victorians* (Manchester and New York: Manchester University Press, 1998), 73–82.

Morgan, Thaïs E., 'Swinburne's Dramatic Monologues: Sex and Ideology', *Victorian Poetry*, 22 (1984), 175–95.

—— 'Mixed Metaphor, Mixed Gender: Swinburne and the Victorian Critics', *Victorian Newsletter*, 73 (1988), 16–19.

—— 'Violence, Creativity and the Feminine: Poetics and Gender Politics in Swinburne and Hopkins', in Antony H. Harrison and Beverly Taylor (eds.), *Gender and Discourse in Victorian Literature and Art* (DeKalb, Ill.: North Illinois Press, 1992), 84–107.

—— 'Male Lesbian Bodies: The Construction of Alternative Masculinities in Courbet, Baudelaire and Swinburne', *Genders*, 15 (Winter 1992), 37–57.

—— 'Reimagining Masculinity in Victorian Criticism: Swinburne and Pater', *Victorian Studies*, 36/3 (1993), 315–32.

—— 'Perverse Male Bodies: Simeon Solomon and Algernon Charles Swinburne', in Peter Horne and Reina Lewis (eds.), *Outlooks: Lesbian and Gay Sexualities and Visual Cultures* (London: Routledge, 1996), 61–85.

Murfin, Ross C., *Swinburne, Hardy, Lawrence and the Burden of Belief* (Chicago and London: University of Chicago Press, 1978). See especially ch. 3: 'Crisis and Transition: Swinburne's *Songs before Sunrise*', 48–78.

Østermark-Johansen, Lene, 'Swinburne's Serpentine Delights: The Aesthetic Critic and the Old Master Drawings in Florence', *Nineteenth-Century Contexts*, 24/1 (2002), 49–72.

Paglia, Camille, 'Swinburne and Pater', in *Sexual Personae: Art and Decadence from Nefertiti to Emily Dickinson* (Harmondsworth: Penguin, 1991), 460–88.

Pease, Allison, 'Questionable Figures: Swinburne's *Poems and Ballads*', *Victorian Poetry*, 35/1 (Spring 1997), 43–56, partly reprised in *Modernism, Mass Culture and the Aesthetics of Obscurity* (Cambridge: Cambridge University Press, 2002), 37–9, 64–71.

Praz, Mario, *The Romantic Agony* (1933), tr. Angus Davidson, 2nd edn. with a foreword by Frank Kermode (Oxford and New York: Oxford University Press, 1970). An early work of scholarship still worth consulting.

Prins, Yopie, 'Swinburne's Sapphic Sublime', in *Victorian Sappho* (Princeton: Princeton University Press, 1998), 112–73. A fine imaginative study of Swinburne's metre.

Reed, John R., 'Swinburne's *Tristram of Lyonesse*: The Poet-Lover's Song of Love', *Victorian Poetry*, 4 (1966), 99–120.

Richardson, James, 'Purity and Pain', ch. 7 in *Vanishing Lives: Style and Self in Tennyson, D. G. Rossetti, Swinburne and Yeats* (Charlottesville, Va.: University Press of Virginia, 1988), 116–36.

Rooksby, Rikky, 'Swinburne in Miniature: A Century of Roundels', *Victorian Poetry*, 23/3 (1985), 249–65.

—— 'Swinburne without Tears: A Guide to the Later Poetry', *Victorian Poetry*, 26/4 (1988), 413–30.

—— 'Upon the Borderlands of Being: Swinburne's Later Elegies', *Victorians Institute Journal*, 20 (1992), 137–58.

—— 'The Algernonicon, or Thirteen Ways of Looking at *Tristram of Lyonesse*', in Rikky Rooksby and Nicholas Shrimpton (eds.), *The Whole Music of Passion: New Essays on Swinburne* (Aldershot: Scolar Press, 1993), 73–91. Good overview of the poem.

Rosenberg, John D., 'Swinburne', *Victorian Studies*, 11 (Dec. 1967), 131–52. A good introductory essay.

Sacks, Peter, 'Swinburne: "Ave Atque Vale" ', in *The English Elegy: Studies in the Genre from Spenser to Yeats* (Baltimore and London: The Johns Hopkins Press, 1985), 204–26. Landmark essay.

Sillars, S. J., 'Tristan and Tristram: Resemblance or Influence?', *Victorian Poetry*, 19 (1981), 81–6.

Snodgrass, Chris, 'Swinburne's Circle of Desire: A Decadent Theme', in Ian Fletcher (ed.), *Decadence and the 1890s* (Stratford-upon-Avon Studies 17; London: Edward Arnold, 1979), 61–87.

Spencer, Robin, 'Whistler, Swinburne and Art for Art's Sake', in Elizabeth Prettejohn (ed.), *After the Pre-Raphaelites: Art and Aestheticism in Victorian England* (Manchester: Manchester University Press, 1999), 59–89.

Staines, David, 'Swinburne's Arthurian World: Swinburne's Arthurian Poetry and its Medieval Sources', *Studia Neophilogica*, 50 (1978), 53–70.

Stevenson, Lionel, 'Algernon Charles Swinburne', in *The Pre-Raphaelite Poets* (Chapel Hill, NC: University of North Carolina Press, 1972), 184–252. Comprehensive overview of Swinburne's life and works with interesting comments about prosody.

Sypher, Francis Jacques, 'Swinburne and Wagner', *Victorian Poetry*, 9 (1971), 165–83.

Tucker, Herbert F., 'Swinburne's *Tristram of Lyonesse* as Assimilationist Epic', in G. Kim Blank and Margot K. Louis (eds.), *Influence and Resistance in Nineteenth-Century English Poetry* (London and Basingstoke: Macmillan, 1993), 76–90.

Vincent, John, 'Flogging is Fundamental: Applications of the Birch in Swinburne's *Lesbia Brandon*', in Eve Kosofsky Sedgwick (ed.), *Novel Gazing: Queer Readings in Fiction* (Durham, NC, and London: Duke University Press, 1997), 269–95.

Wagner-Lawlor, Jennifer, ' "Yet many of these are askew": On Imitation, Originality, and Parody in Swinburne's *Heptalogia*', *Victorian Literature and Culture*, 26/2 (1998), 237–57.

Zonana, Joyce, 'Swinburne's Sappho: The Muse as Sister-Goddess', *Victorian Poetry*, 28 (1990), 39–51.

Index